WHEN FREEDOM IS THE QUESTION, ABOLITION IS THE ANSWER

WHEN FREEDOM IS THE QUESTION, ABOLITION IS THE ANSWER

REFLECTIONS ON COLLECTIVE LIBERATION

BILL AYERS

BEACON PRESS, BOSTON

BEACON PRESS
Boston, Massachusetts
www.beacon.org

Beacon Press books
are published under the auspices of
the Unitarian Universalist Association of Congregations.

27 26 25 24   8 7 6 5 4 3 2 1

This book is printed on acid-free paper that meets the uncoated paper
ANSI/NISO specifications for permanence as revised in 1992.

Text design and composition by Kim Arney

Library of Congress Cataloging-in-Publication Data is available for this title.
ISBN: 978-0-8070-2034-0; e-book: 978-0-8070-2035-7;
audiobook: 978-0-8070-1718-0

To the memory of Malik Alim, freedom fighter and comrade,
brother and friend. Your life was short, too short,
but it was a full life nonetheless—you lived so fiercely,
with such urgency, and at full attention.
Your community carries on, now and always,
in your reflected light.

CONTENTS

AUTHOR'S NOTE

These essays emerge from a podcast I created in 2019 with my comrade and friend Malik Alim from the Let Us Breathe Collective and Black Lives Matter! in Chicago. I learned everything from Malik as we moved steadily from a kind of makeshift backyard clubhouse production into a more grounded space in which we've engaged today's freedom fighters in reflecting on the meaning of that dynamic, elusive, and promising word *freedom*. The podcast is called *Under the Tree: A Seminar on Freedom*.

On our podcast we imagine ourselves to be a small but energetic insurgent community, or an underground school-without-walls working to understand and engage the concept of freedom in this political moment. In an infinite and expanding universe, our knowledge is finite, and not-knowing is the default for each of us. We struggle to open our eyes, to study and to learn, to interrogate the world as it is, and to work toward a world with more joy and more justice for all. We resist those who traffic in ignorance, anyone who willfully tramples on facts and data and evidence. So, there are really no dumb questions. Whose interests are served, after all, when we fail to ask dumb or difficult questions, or when we are left in the dark about this fact or that particular information? For example, why is the US 2023 National Defense Authorization Act a monstrous $847 billion—more than the world's next nine defense budgets combined?[1] That's over 65 percent of discretionary US dollars spent on a hypermilitarized budget. Meanwhile, over half a million people are unhoused in the US, one in ten adults is in "significant" medical debt, almost 17 percent of American children live in poverty, and, with under 5 percent of the world's population, the US cages over 20 percent of the world's prisoners.[2] So . . . if you don't know, now you know. And keep asking.

What is freedom? How do we get free? What are the freedom dreams that encourage us and drive us forward? If we're blinded to the social reality we're swimming through, who benefits? Where are we on the clock of the universe, and what does the known demand of us now? These questions animate our every conversation and our ongoing reflection. We're bound together by our collective commitment to look at the world as if it could be otherwise and then to get busy in projects of resistance and repair—and, yes, of revolution.

We lost Malik, twenty-eight years old, in a tragic accident, on August 20, 2021, and every step we've taken since has been in his memory, and with his guidance.

Under the Tree is a metaphor meant to signal that, when the topic is liberation, the classroom or workshop can come to life anywhere: a park or a house of worship, a storefront or the street, a hiring hall or a factory floor, a people's assembly or a demonstration, or—why not?—a comfortable piece of ground in the shade of a big old tree. Wherever folks come together to face one another authentically, without pretenses, in order to take stock of the world as it is and to wonder about how we might build a world that should be or could be, that becomes another site of learning and growth and change.

We draw inspiration and wisdom from the Freedom Schools created during the great uprisings of the 1950s and 1960s. Those fugitive spaces were sites where people gathered to organize an insurgency, and in those settings—modern expressions of the centuries-old Black Freedom Movement, rising today in astonishing new ways—to urgently interrogate the circumstances of their lives, to name their political moment, and to think freely toward a world built on the twin pillars of love and justice. Freedom School participants generated their own questions, and over time a practice evolved that steadily unlocked the wisdom in the room, built agency and empowerment through engaging the real problems people faced in their lives, including structural barriers and obstacles, that led to shared inquiry and then to collective action. Each of the eight Reflections that follow adopt a rhythm that's been a feature of my teaching for as long as I can remember, and that has become the standard frame for each episode of the podcast: I begin with a poem which is "our moment of Zen," an opportunity to close our eyes, breathe deeply, let our analytical minds click off for a moment as we get started. I want to remind us of the centrality of the arts and of humanism as principle, guide, and source in all our pursuits—our lives as humans, our efforts as citizens and residents, our projects as workers and creators. Poet Jane Hirshfield writes, "Great poetry is not a donkey carrying obedient sentiment in pretty forms, it is a bird of prey tearing open whatever needs to be opened."[3] And Langston Hughes invents an entire vocabulary to underline the potential of poetry to illuminate, to educate, and to nourish our humanity:

> Poetry possesses the power of worriation. Poetry can both delight and disturb. It can interest folks. It can upset folks. Poetry can convey both pleasure and pain. And poetry can make people think. If poetry makes people think, it might make them think constructive thoughts, even thoughts about how to change themselves, their town and their state for the better. Some poems, like many of the great verses in the Bible, can make people think about changing all mankind, even the whole world. Poems, like prayers, possess power.[4]

The poem is followed by a "writing prompt" which is a kind of provocation that asks readers to gather their thoughts in anticipation of actively engaging what's to come. No one comes to a class or a book as a blank slate or an empty vessel, so everyone should be ready to pitch in and join the fray. The prompts invite active engagement and effort in the spirit of Walt Whitman's admonition to readers that "the process of reading is not a half sleep, but, in the highest sense an exercise, a gymnast's struggle; that the reader is to do something for himself, must be on the alert, must himself or herself construct indeed the poem, argument, history, metaphysical essay—the text furnishing the hints, the clue, the start or framework. Not the book needs so much to be the complete thing, but the reader of the book does."[5] Through the prompts I'm asking you to be on the alert, and to wrestle with each and every argument and idea.

We've been honored again and again to be in conversation with artists, activists, authors, and academics—in a segment we call "AAAAH," pronounced as a sigh—who've thought deeply about the question of freedom, engaged personally in the freedom struggles, and profoundly influenced my own thinking, among them Juan Gonzalez, Barbara Ransby, Mariame Kaba, Robin D. G. Kelley, adrienne maree brown, Lisa Lee, Ash-Lee Woodard Henderson, Rashid Khalidi, Daphne Muse, Bernardine Dohrn, Alec Karakatsanis, David Stovall, Alice Kim, Kathy Boudin, Crystal Laura, Adam Bush, Kevin Kumashiro, Brian Jones, Chesa Boudin, Eleanor Stein, Beth Richie, Prexy Nesbitt, Jeff Jones, Robert Shetterly, Katherine Franke, Dima Khalidi, Aislinn Pulley, Bill Fletcher Jr., Joel Westheimer, Kari Kokka, Rochelle Gutierrez, Jay Gillen, Timmy Chau, Kristiana Rae Colon, Ryan Alexander-Tanner, Stacey Sutton, Wayne Au, Howard Waitzkin, Renaldo Hudson, Raynard Sanders, Aaron Dixon, Heather Booth, Maya Schenwar, Rachel Wallis, Victoria Law, Sharbreon Plummer, Xavier McElrath-Bey, Therese Quinn, Claire Kiefer, Martha Swan, Peggy Shepherd, Cliff Mayotte, Dave Zirin, Dorothy Burge, Flint Taylor, Kevin Kumashiro, Helen Shiller, Roxanne Dunbar-Ortiz, Theodore Richards, Walter Riley, Zayd Dohrn, Tara Betts, Tongo Eisen-Martin, Erica Meiners, Marshan Allen, Stephanie Skora, Susan Mills, Denzel Burke, Destine Phillips, Tommy Hagan, Beth Awano, Eliza Gonring, Danny Katch, Michael Fischer, Zoharah Simmons, Michael Simmons, Dan Berger, Jon Melrod, Randolph Stone, Rick Ayers, Fida Jiryis, Greg King, Damon Williams, Daniel Kisslinger, Leif Carlson, Will Harling, Claire Dederer, Haley Pessin, Anthony Arnove, Vinnie Schiraldi, Janie Paul, Mneesha Gelman, Astra Taylor, and Eve Ewing.

Respect!

—January 2024

LAND AND SPACE
ACKNOWLEDGMENT

As a future ancestor, I'm writing from the so-called Chicagoland area of Illinois, a conundrum wrapped in a contradiction—both a confirmation and a crime scene. Sometimes I imagine Chicago wrapped in that distinctive yellow crime-scene tape: "Do Not Enter. Criminal Investigation Underway."

These lands were stewarded for millennia by many Indigenous peoples and lineages, including the Potawatomi, the Ojibwe, and the Odawa, as well as the Menominee, Miami, Ho-Chunk, Sac, and Fox nations. Here, these human beings raised their children, created their communities, made sense and meaning of their lives for one another, experienced the flowing and the passing of their time together, planned for the future, and buried their dead. I acknowledge them and thank them all; I apologize for the actions of my settler-colonial forebearers; and I join in solidarity in seeking truth, repair, and reconciliation.

Chicago's name, derived from the Algonquian language, means "river whose shores are lined with wild leeks." I note that, following the settler violence culminating in the Blackhawk War of 1832, Indigenous peoples were murdered or forcibly removed from these lands. Over a century later, under a different set of oppressive policies, many were once again coerced to migrate, this time back to the urban centers where their ancestors had earlier been robbed and forced out against their will. Chicago now has one of the largest Indigenous urban populations in the US, with more than sixty-five thousand Native Americans in the greater metropolitan area.

Chicago is also the home of the first non-native naturalized citizen of the Potawatomi people, Jean Baptiste Point du Sable, a man of African descent who is considered the first permanent non-Indigenous settler in the area. Sometimes referred to as the "Founder of Chicago," Du Sable lived here with his wife, Kitihawa, a Potawatomi woman he married in 1770. When Kitihawa was removed from her home by the US government as part of a series of forced displacements, du Sable followed her and their two children to Iowa, where they raised their family together.

Chicago is a confluence of water, wildness, peoples, hopes, and aspirations, a place of outsized and crazy complexity, built up by the hands of immigrant workers and African-ancestored people escaping terror and the afterlife of slavery during the Great Migration. Justice seekers, freedom fighters, teachers and cultural workers, artists and creators, organizers and activists—all of us who stand on humanity's freedom side remember and honor a history of stolen land and resources, genocide and exploitation, and we pledge to keep our eyes and our hearts open in our shared struggle for peace and repair, justice and joy, balance and love.

Chicago is where I reside and work, where I rise up filled with gratitude and awe on each fresh morning. This is where I recommit to projects of repair and revolution in this bruised and battered world. Chicago is where I begin again.

1

WHEN FREEDOM
IS THE QUESTION . . .

Oh, freedom
Oh, freedom
Oh, freedom over me
And before I'd be a slave I'd be buried in-a my grave (oh, yes)
And I'd fight for my right to be free.

M ake a list of five words like freedom—words that spark in your mind in the wake or the echo of that one propulsive word, *freedom*. Write a sentence or two about whatever images, ideas, and thoughts each word presents or awakens in you. Now write about the concept of freedom itself, its depth and dimensions, boundaries and borders, its ambitions and longings and essential features. Take a moment to scratch out a few notes before you read any further.

— REFLECTION ONE: FREEDOM DEMANDS ACTION —

This is a good moment to reflect once more on the question of freedom—to explore its history and to illuminate its dimensions, to investigate where we are and to wonder about where we might go next. The word *freedom* is practically appliquéd on our American minds—we're born free in the freest country on earth, we're told repeatedly, and it seems that individuals and corporations alike, people from the far left to the reactionary right, embrace freedom as a positive force and a trumpeted value in some vague and general sense—the sanctimonious Freedom Caucus, the opportunistic Freedom Unlimited Card from Chase Bank, *The Courage to Be Free* by the insufferable Ron

DeSantis, or the electrifying Black Freedom Movement. What does anyone mean by *freedom* in particular? The answer is difficult to pin down, but let's try anyway.

The moment can feel like the absolute worst of times: a new and escalating cold war with China; a hot and destructive proxy war in Europe and a preannounced genocide against the Palestinian people of Gaza underway; raging, racialized police violence unchecked; environmental collapse on full display; fragile and often anemic democratic institutions on life support; religious authoritarianism on the rise; women's bodily integrity under sustained assault. The overlapping crises threaten to overwhelm us.

But on a different day, or from a different angle of regard, these days can feel like the best of times—twenty-six million people took to the streets in 2020 in response to the police murder of George Floyd, the largest public outpouring for racial justice in history; women across a wide political spectrum have refused to accept a medieval definition of their rights; labor has won historic, game-changing victories, from the Writers Guild of America to the United Auto Workers, and from Amazon to Starbucks; and broad forces are on the march worldwide to resist plunder and extraction and to preserve life on earth. I wake up every day and glance at poet Mary Oliver's words taped to the wall, capturing a sense of this universal contradiction: "Just to be alive on this fresh morning in the broken world."[1]

Charles Dickens would recognize our contemporary predicament at once: the winter of despair and the spring of hope; an age of foolishness and an age of wisdom; darkness in mortal combat with light. Dickens understood that life is never one thing in isolation from every other thing. Yes, there is exploitation, but there is also resistance; progress, yes, and also backlash. More than one thing is happening at once. If we freeze our focus or draw the frame too rigidly, we miss the noisy, dynamic, frenetic magnificence of life as it's actually happening.

So I want to expand and redraw the boundaries of how I see and think about freedom as well as the reality that spreads out before us, the world that we encounter every day. I want to rethink where one thing ends and another thing begins, of where to look and what to look for.

"Ah, contradiction," writes Viet Thanh Nguyen. "The perpetual body odor of humanity!"[2]

Freedom as a living thing and a vital aspiration is partially revealed when we look unblinkingly into the face of *unfreedom:* if unfreedom includes being prevented from voting, then freedom must *involve* the act of voting; if unfreedom is in part being forced to attend underfunded, segregated, miseducating schools, freedom *embraces* integrating into the privileged schools and fighting for an honest curriculum; if unfreedom is having no roof over your family's head, freedom includes having access to adequate housing; if unfreedom is policies and politics of caging and cruelty, exclusion and dehumanization, then freedom must unlock the cages and *abolish* those heartless practices. Freedom in fact is always freedom in opposition.

"Freedom Now!" was the call to arms of the celebrated Black Freedom Movement in the 1950s and 1960s, the massive social justice movement that generated real social change as well as a language, a philosophy, and a vast soundtrack that contingently defined (and then continually reimagined and redefined) the meaning of freedom. "We Shall Overcome," a Christian hymn reworked by Guy Carawan at the Highlander Folk School in Tennessee, became the movement's anthem. "Oh, Freedom," "We Shall Not Be Moved," and "Woke Up This Morning with My Mind Stayed on Freedom"—popular tunes easily learned by people while marching or picketing—were the brilliant creations of the Freedom Singers.

The Freedom Singers were born as a student quartet in Georgia in the early 1960s. They generated and popularized a turbulent, rushing stream of freedom songs, and they quickly became a project and a pillar of the Student Nonviolent Coordinating Committee (SNCC), the militant youth wing of the movement. These new abolitionists were notably impatient for justice—they led the Freedom Rides on interstate buses, the lunch counter sit-ins in the Deep South, and direct-action protests across the land. The Freedom Singers were in the fray, and they built the musical canon from the ground up—field shouts and church music, gospel hymns and traditional folk tunes, catchy jingles and propulsive African rhythms. The communal singing that characterized their approach, a mingling of a cappella church performances with protest songs, became a major educational tool of the civil rights movement all over the world, as well as an empowering ritual for the activists. Before every demonstration or protest or action, we gathered, joined hands, and sang at the top of our lungs to make ourselves bigger and stronger than we actually were, and to chase away that cunning, disarming demon—fear. And when we confronted a barrier—sitting in or standing up, marching or picketing—and the police troops moved in, folks spontaneously once more broke into song: "I Ain't A-Scared of Your Jail 'Cause I Want My Freedom." We were riding on a "freedom high," which gave us a certain superhuman strength, and, paradoxically, a certain adrenaline-clouded judgment.

At the 1963 March on Washington for Jobs and Freedom, where Martin Luther King Jr. gave his iconic "I Have a Dream" speech, John Lewis, the twenty-three-year-old chairman of SNCC and later the legendary congressman from Georgia, declared, "We do not want our freedom gradually, but we want to be free now! . . . We are tired of being beaten by policemen. We are tired of seeing our people locked up in jail over and over again. . . . Wake up America! Wake up!"[3] On that note, the Freedom Singers were joined on the steps of the Lincoln Memorial by Marian Anderson, the first African American singer to perform at the Metropolitan Opera, who was celebrated around the world for an open-air concert she had given on these same steps in 1939 in protest over being banned by the Daughters of the American Revolution from singing to an integrated audience earlier that year; the renowned gospel singer Mahalia Jackson; the popular folk singer, actor, and activist Theodore Bikel; and rising folk stars Odetta, Bob Dylan, Joan Baez, and Peter, Paul, and Mary. Their music lifted the marchers and inspired the movement, and soon freedom songs spread like a prairie fire, carrying the message rapidly across the country and impacting folk and rock and commercial popular music for decades: Marvin Gaye's "What's Going On," Curtis Mayfield's "Keep on Pushing,'" Sam Cooke's "A Change Is Gonna Come," the Staple Singers' "Freedom Highway," James Brown's "Say It Loud, I'm Black and I'm Proud," Bob Dylan's "Only a Pawn in Their Game," Nina Simone's "Mississippi Goddam," Bob Marley and the Wailers' "Get Up, Stand Up," the Neville Brothers' "Wake Up," Rage Against the Machine's "Freedom," and thousands more. The sounds of freedom were in the community—and on the air.

In the wake of the Black Freedom Movement a liberating spirit was loosed in the land, unleashing freedom's energy, and a new world heaved into view. Everything felt like music, and the music felt like freedom. Abolishing all forms of subjugation became the agenda and pushed forward. A next wave of women's liberation rose up in a surge of grassroots truth-telling; Puerto Rican independence seemed suddenly possible; American Indian Movement warriors organized and stood tall for their people's freedom; gay liberation, Chicano liberation, and disability rights were all at once on the move, and in the mix. Freedom dreams were contagious and, in today's terms, "going viral."

This was, of course, not the first time the idea of freedom animated complex conversations and earth-shaking events in the US. For all their contradictions and contested meanings, the American Revolution, the Civil War, Reconstruction, and more also rode that freedom highway. Neither was it the first time the sounds of freedom were expressed in song—social movements from the labor movement to the trans movement and every stop in between unfailingly generated a soundtrack of resistance and revolt. The original abolitionists rallied around the freedom song "Get off the Track" in the 1840s, and enslaved people, denied the luxury of open protest, transformed field hollers and biblical verses into music to spread the news on the common wind, perhaps most famously Exodus 5.1, "Go Down Moses" ("and let my people go"). Union troops marched into battle singing "John Brown's Body," which emerged from the oral tradition of camp meetings, improvised singing learned and passed on by rote and that evolved into the "Battle Hymn of the Republic." But the musical accompaniment of this Third American Revolution was so rich and so varied—it spread so far and ran so deep—that it brought forth a fresh idea of freedom and embedded that idea deep into the popular culture.

Today's movement music rises on that legacy and comes into the world rapid-fire. Here's the chorus of the Puerto Rican singer and freedom fighter Taina Asili's "Abolition":

> We call for abolition / Cuz' we know police and prisons / Were made with a single mission / A racist, oppressive system / So, we work for abolition / Cuz' we walk in the tradition / Of those who carried a vision / To take us to liberation / So we work for abolition / Abolition / Abolition / Abolition / We work for abolition[4]

The movement was providing a practical syllabus, too—a kind of roadmap for a widespread popular education project on freedom that reached into schools and houses of worship, neighborhoods and communities, factories and farms, workplaces and businesses. The chants were audible and galvanizing—"What do we want? Freedom! When do we want it? NOW!"—and the movement was blazingly conspicuous, on full display for all to see.

Like Cuba's nationwide literacy campaign at that time, Paulo Freire's groundbreaking adult education projects in rural Brazil, among other popular education efforts, the method was hands-on—learning by doing—the pedagogy was relational and communal, and the curriculum was based on asking big questions, and then posing problems for inquiry, dialogue, discussion, and action. These problems had no simple solutions; these questions, no pat or easy answers. Why are we in the freedom movement? Let's talk about that. What do we want? Let's dig deep, and then deeper and deeper. What is freedom, anyway, and how do we get free? Let's dream a little—OK, now let's dream bigger and reach further.

Embedded in each question was a message: the people with the problems are also the people with the solutions. But in order to activate and find answers, people must develop a growing sense of their own agency, their own power, and their own possibilities, and they must come to see the situation before them as transient, not fixed. Freire wrote that the oppressed "must perceive the reality of oppression not as a closed world from which there is no exit, but as a limiting situation which they can transform."[5] The big idea was change—personal, political, historical, and social. Freedom.

The movement initially created what educator-organizer Jay Gillen calls *crawl spaces*—the alleys and margins where people can mobilize, organize, and come together as authentic and reliable, in order to think for themselves about what had been before now forbidden: Why are schools and communities segregated by race? Why do some people live this kind of life, and others that other kind? What causes poverty? Who creates wealth? Who owns the land? Who deserves a decent life? Why do Black people live shorter lives than white people? Why can't I vote? Why is the US seemingly always at war—serial invaders and occupiers of other sovereign nations? Why, why, why? And then, each and every time: What are we going to do about it?

And, of course, from these crawl spaces, a working description/interpretation of freedom emerged, enacted in the streets and carried with the music and the culture. That characterization was not fixed or finished, but was—as always—dynamic, lively, and open-ended, a work in progress just like each of us. We knew that a vital operating interpretation is not the same as an inert dictionary definition; we thought of *freedom* as a verb, not a noun, and to think of freedom that way was to resist conducting a postmortem on a static concept or performing an autopsy on a lifeless idea. Freedom is a practice—it's vitalized in day-to-day action: the quiet preparation, and the urgent thrust. Because the movement was moving, the streets alive with struggle, we knew that freedom was not an idle dream. Freedom, in the words of the contemporary activist Kelly Hayes, was "a fire that's burning in real time. And the blaze is spreading."[6]

"Words like freedom," to borrow from Langston Hughes, became active expressions of desire and resolve: to liberate, to rise up, to overturn, to rebel, to abolish, to make a revolution—a "revolution in values" as the Reverend Martin Luther King Jr. advocated long ago, in order to make a revolution in fact.[7] Freedom![8]

Identifying unfreedom carried with it a moral imperative—the responsibility to act. "Don't just sit there," Nina Simone instructed from the stage at the Summer of Soul concert in Harlem in 1969. "For God's sake, do something." Freedom was an achievement to be won, not a gift to be bestowed. It had no direct link to charity; it was not a grant from a philanthropic foundation nor the largesse of some ostentatious benefactor—let's call him a "Gentleman Bountiful," to queer the sexist image of his better-known sister Lady Bountiful, with her perfumed hankies. Freedom was to be seized rather than received. And that's as true now as it was then.

So freedom was tied to protest and resistance, to community-building and solidarity, to collectively identifying the barriers to one's humanity and then struggling arm in arm, and heart to heart, to overcome those obstacles. Freedom was neither a stable nor a passive state of being but an active state of engagement; freedom was something to be accomplished in dialogue and struggle with others. Freedom pointed toward personal fulfillment, yes, but in the dynamic, ongoing development of sisterhood and brotherhood: community action and collective liberation.

The dream of freedom has animated countless revolutions and justice movements the world around. It surely breathed life into every anticolonial and anti-imperialist struggle throughout the world in the twentieth century. The people of Guinea-Bissau, Angola, Mozambique, and South African, the Vietnamese and the Cubans—all were rising up, *doing something*, with freedom on their minds, and, in their minds, freedom was the recognition of necessity.

A telling example from our own not-so-distant history is the abolitionist movement leading up to the Civil War. Abraham Lincoln gave his First Inaugural Address in 1861 as the winds of war and secession blew hot and hard across the land—this is the speech that schoolchildren *never* read because it's so tortured and so distant from the mythologized image of Honest Abe Lincoln, the liberator, that the country desperately wants to embrace. "I have no purpose," Lincoln told Congress and the country, "directly or indirectly, to interfere with the institution of slavery in the States where it exists. I believe I have no lawful right to do so, and I have no inclination to do so."⁹ Say what? You have no inclination to interfere with the institution of slavery? What a disappointment you are, Abe!

The main energy for abolition was being generated by the enslaved people themselves, who were creating a crisis and driving a movement. Resistance and rebellion were, of course, constant within the regime of slavery—a phenomenon that the rulers had to continually account for as the common cost of doing their dirty business—but slave revolts were now occurring in accelerating cycles of unrest throughout the eighteenth century. Enslaved workers were self-liberating in every direction, and then, in 1791, thousands of African slaves rose up on the island of Hispaniola under the leadership of Toussaint L'Ouverture and fought for their freedom against their French masters. In one of the most significant social revolutions in world history, the Haitians liberated themselves from France and abolished slavery in 1804. In 1802, William Wordsworth wrote a poem to the revolutionary leader called "To Toussaint L'Ouverture" that ends with these lines: "Thy friends are exultations, agonies, / And love, and man's unconquerable mind."¹⁰

The impact of the Haitian Revolution was immediate and severe: a cauldron of insurrection swept the land, and subversive stories circulated with speed and momentum from runaways and maroons and sailors and smugglers until they reached every port and city along the Atlantic. The slavocracy in the US was set back on its heels, freaking out. Abolitionists were on the march, with Harriet Tubman and Frederick Douglass setting the moral tone in the starkest possible terms, and with John Brown and his freedom fighters already martyred at Harpers Ferry in 1859. The abolitionist movement pressed relentlessly forward without hesitation or compromise, *doing something* and creating an ethical imperative and eventually an irresistible force for emancipation and for abolition. The enslaved resistance and the abolitionist campaigns fanned the embers of freedom from below, massive disruption and disturbance kept rising, and, by the time the flames blew into a firestorm, Lincoln responded.

Abraham Lincoln's Second Inaugural Address—the one available in most history textbooks—was delivered two years after the Emancipation Proclamation, and his words could easily have flowed from the pen of the towering abolitionist Frederick Douglass (*and perhaps they did*): "[The war will] continue until all the wealth piled by the bondsman's two hundred and fifty years of unrequited toil shall be sunk, and until every drop of blood drawn with the lash shall be paid by another drawn with the sword."[11] This was the angry cry of abolition, retribution, and reparations, the real stakes in the conflict, which was defined by the heroism and sacrifice of the striking and self-liberating enslaved people, and the soldiers fighting, for once, on their side. And these words are important to remember today, almost 160 years on, as we continue to raise the specter of abolition and the demand for reparations for years of unrequited toil—with interest.

But note that freedom, and fundamental social change, never comes from the good intentions or sudden awakenings of the powerful. It always rises from the bottom—fire from below. Lincoln was shaken awake by the rebels and pushed forward into action by the gathering storm. And that might remind us that, in the thousands-year history of organized states, only in the last couple of hundred years has any state extended the zone of human freedom a single iota—and then only when driven by massive upheaval, action, and red-hot fire from the margin to the center and from the ground up.

Freedom lovers and movement builders, activists and organizers, abolitionists and revolutionaries—and eventually masses of people in motion—brought us the end of slavery, and later the dawn of the eight-hour day, women's suffrage, Social Security, disabled people's rights, women's reproductive freedom, public education, civil rights, clean air and water, queer rights, and more. None of this was accomplished without conflict or contestation, and, of course, the ground of struggle was the culture as well as the streets, the factories, and the workplaces, the courts and the schools, traditional politics as well as irregular warfare. There was never a single moment nor a perfect target to strike; the freedom movement was always complex and layered, quilted together by real people acting independently and in harmony.

Think for a moment about the abolitionist activists of 1840. They wrote articles and manifestos against slavery; they made arguments and held meetings, mobilized demonstrations, developed strategies and deployed a wide range of tactics. They organized for abolition. Their opposition to slavery meant that they were a small minority, and it put them in opposition to the Founders, the Constitution, the law, the Bible, their preachers, and their parents. There was no way they could have known that a mere twenty-five years later the slavocracy would fall as a result of their spade work and a bloody civil war. But it did, and that should give us a bit of perspective on our own work here and now.

We can all imagine what we would have done so long ago when history was being made: we'd have built the Underground Railroad, sat-in at the lunch counters, marched across the Selma bridge. In another context we'd have joined the Paris Commune, and, in another, we'd have sheltered and protected Anne Frank. But it's too easy to know what to do in the past, much harder to choose a path looking forward—and without any guarantees.

No one can escape their era. There may well have been better times to fight the power, but now is our one and only time—we will have no other. Yes, life is a challenge, and there are no commandments to follow, no essence to achieve. But the void before us is also a horizon of infinite possibilities. Now's our chance, because history is always being made and every moment is "historic." History has surprised us before, and it will again. We can each choose to be a part of that surprise.

Frederick Douglass lived through the abolition of slavery and the flowering of Black Reconstruction only to witness the reestablishment of the structures of white power and the rise of the KKK. What did he do in the gathering dread and darkness? He certainly did not crumble from "protest fatigue" or the lack of a convenient on-ramp for the struggle; he got up, dusted himself off, and set out once more to organize a mighty justice movement from the bottom up.

Our job, right here and right now, is to become today's abolitionists—reimagining, resisting, and rebuilding in the name of freedom. The guitar wizard and freedom fighter Tommy Morello urges us to "let freedom ring" in large and small ways, and remember, too, the words of Taina Asili: "Freedom is a journey, it is not a sprint/ This is a process, not just a single event."[12] Abolition can mean a campaign or a project or a movement to tear down a single institution or wall or structure; what I have in mind can certainly embrace the specific or the singular case, but it's also broader, more extensive, and much more inclusive—abolition as a complete politics. In this sense, abolition is the repudiation and nullification of oppression everywhere, and the struggle against subjugation anywhere: abuse or cruelty of any trace or tone, exploitation in any context.

An aspect of abolition is eradication or removal, true. But the more challenging and more rewarding task of abolition is the work of creation: the building of institutions and relationships, structures and cultures that would make slavery unthinkable, and then prisons and police unnecessary, and exploitation obsolete. Abolition, in the words of Fred Moten and Stefano Harney, is "the founding of a new society," because abolition eliminates a society that could have slavery (or prisons or police), and builds a society where slavery is impossible.[13] World-building, then, is the true vocation of abolitionists, and, while we don't and can't know exactly what replaces it, the aspiration, the struggle, and the process is all we have to lead us to the answer. Freedom is the horizon.

2

A WORLD THAT COULD BE—
BUT IS NOT YET

This is the year that squatters evict landlords,
gazing like admirals from the rail
of the roof deck
or levitating hands in praise
of steam in the shower;
this is the year
that shawled refugees deport judges
who stare at the floor
and their swollen feet
as files are stamped
with their destination;
this is the year that police revolvers,
stove-hot, blister the fingers
of raging cops,
and nightsticks splinter
in their palms;
this is the year that dark skinned men
lynched a century ago
return to sip coffee quietly
with the apologizing descendants
of their executioners.

This is the year that those
who swim the border's undertow
and shiver in boxcars
are greeted with trumpets and drums
at the first railroad crossing
on the other side;
this is the year that the hands
pulling tomatoes from the vine
uproot the deed to the earth that sprouts
the vine,
the hands canning tomatoes
are named in the will
that owns the bedlam of the cannery;

this is the year that the eyes stinging from the poison that purifies toilets
awaken at last to the sight
of a rooster-loud hillside,
pilgrimage of immigrant birth; this is the year that cockroaches
become extinct, that no doctor
finds a roach embedded
in the ear of an infant;
this is the year that the food stamps
of adolescent mothers
are auctioned like gold doubloons,
and no coin is given to buy machetes
for the next bouquet of severed heads
in coffee plantation country.

If the abolition of slave-manacles
began as a vision of hands without manacles, then this is the year;
if the shutdown of extermination camps
began as imagination of a land
without barbed wire or the crematorium,
then this is the year;
if every rebellion begins with the idea
that conquerors on horseback are not many-legged gods, that they too drown
if plunged in the river,
then this is the year.

So may every humiliated mouth,
teeth like desecrated headstones,
fill with the angels of bread.

—MARTÍN ESPADA

Write ten lines or sentences, each beginning with the phrase "This is the year." Resist the temptation to make a list of New Year's resolutions: "This is the year I exercise more and eat better"; "This is the year I smoke less (or more) weed"; "This is the year I listen more carefully to my partner." Rather, in the spirit of Martín Espada's epic poem, identify and point to some political/historical wrongs and then imagine reversing or abolishing those injustices.

— REFLECTION TWO: FREEDOM'S PARADOX —

At the 1968 Democratic Party Convention in Chicago, I was arrested
with an unruly mass of other people in a chaotic street fight with the
police on Michigan Avenue. Packed into a crowded police van rushing
headlong toward Cook County Jail, I was, somewhat oddly, filled with
energy and hope—in fact, I felt a little ecstatic. It was the strangest
thing, that feeling, and it puzzled me. We had not backed down, true,
and we had not run away; we had stood up for peace and for freedom,
and we'd conveyed our urgent message to a vast audience. On the other
hand, I was bloodied and bruised, wounded and hurting. The whole
world was watching that night, and in that dark and stuffy van, holding
a rag to my bleeding head, I felt myself breathing the refreshing air of
freedom as if for the first time.

This paradox lies at the very heart of freedom: We are perhaps
most free when we're standing in front of an imposing wall, naming
a roadblock to our own (or to our neighbor's) full humanity and then
throwing ourselves against that obstacle. The moment may appear
obstructed or fraught or frightening or dangerous—it may, in fact, be
all of those things at once. And yet freedom pitches into view precisely
when *unfreedom* is identified (enslavement, subjugation, abuse, cruelty,
persecution, extraction, exploitation, oppression), and we reach for a
sledgehammer to break through that savage wall, shoulder to shoulder
with others in an effort to prevail over unfreedom. Fred Moten says
that freedom dreams were born in the dark and deadly hold of a slave
ship. And Henry David Thoreau, speaking to his friend Emerson from
a jail cell, famously said that prison was "the only house in a slave State
in which a free man can abide with honor."[1] In prison, yet somehow
free. Identifying and naming injustice, organizing and agitating against
it in the company of your chosen family, uniting in love in order to
breach barricades and overcome barriers—that's where freedom ex-
plodes onto the scene and comes to life as three-dimensional, vivid,
trembling, and real.

Frederick Douglass describes a moment when he refused to allow
himself to be beaten by his master's son and, risking death, fought

back. Without any assurances of success, Douglass battled the man to a standoff and defended himself successfully, intentionally refraining from the sweet temptation to beat his attacker to a pulp. Amazingly, Douglass was not punished; perhaps the young man felt humiliated and wanted to simply walk away. In any case, when he reflected on the encounter later, Douglass wrote, "I was *nothing before; I was a man now.* . . . After resisting him, I felt as I had never felt before. It was resurrection. . . . I had reached the point where I was not afraid to die. This spirit made me a freeman in fact. When a slave cannot be flogged, he is more than half free."[2]

Douglass had expressed himself openly, fully, and authentically; he had removed the servile and affable mask of compliance by fighting back. He had openly named unfreedom, resisted it, and felt suddenly resurrected—exhilarated, intoxicated, energized. Although still enslaved, Douglass had tasted freedom. Freedom in action. That's a clear statement of the paradox, the basic contradiction, and the mystery: the "freedom" of sitting on the couch smoking a joint (don't get me wrong, that's not a bad thing in itself) is an anemic illusion next to the radiant freedom of punching your master in the nose.

There's a scene in Stanley Nelson's brilliant 2015 documentary film, *The Black Panther Party: Vanguard of the Revolution,* that knocked me off my chair when my wife, Bernardine; my brother Rick; and I first saw it, and it's stayed with me ever since. Nelson interviewed a few Panthers—Gil Parker, Muhammad Mubarak, Roland Freeman, and Wayne Pharr—who had survived a murderous assault on the Panther headquarters by the Los Angeles police in 1970. The Panthers described what it was like to be under the full brunt of state violence, trading gunshots with the police for hours and suffering multiple wounds. They were fairly certain that they were all going to die. Then Wayne Pharr surprised Nelson, saying: "I felt free. I felt absolutely free. I was a free Negro. I was making my own rules. You couldn't get in and I couldn't get out." But for those few hours, according to Pharr, "I was a free Negro."[3] There were no assurances that the Panthers would win, of course, nor that they would move the needle forward even a notch in the centuries-old struggle for Black liberation. There was no certainty that anyone would walk away from the police assault alive. Still, Wayne Pharr claims that for those few hours he *felt free*.

Wayne Pharr had joined the Panthers to act against white supremacist structures and practices that he'd concluded held him back or pushed him down as a human being—the police as a brutalizing occupation force in particular. These were injustices to oppose because they created concrete barriers to his and his people's fulfillment. By naming them as obstacles, he focused attention on them as things to defy and defeat, to live beyond into an imagined and more humane future. Joining the Panthers was acting in freedom, and, arm in arm with others, he was taking on the responsibility of abolishing the offenses—reinventing himself, and now naming himself as an agent of liberation. Choosing with others to be a freedom fighter and acting on that choice, he found some notable measure of self-determination: "I was a free Negro."

When speaking of her unique perspective on freedom, the philosopher Maxine Greene evokes the memory of Rene Char, a poet and a member of the Resistance during the German occupation of France in the 1940s. Char and his comrades were unwilling to live peacefully in a world that offended their sense of justice and disrupted their lives, so they refused to submit—they chose instead to build an illegal underground organization. Good for them. And, just as with Wayne Pharr and his comrades, just as with Frederick Douglass, their refusal contained no promise of success. Still, risking their lives to challenge the catastrophe unfolding before their eyes felt to them like the only way they could live fully and freely and was, therefore, the correct and urgent thing to do. Acting against invasion and occupation, against fascism, pointed to the possibility of change and announced to any who would look or listen that another world was possible. In the most difficult and dire conditions—Nazis in control, troops marching overhead, danger in every direction—Rene Char described being visited by an "apparition of freedom."[4] Like Frederick Douglass and Wayne Pharr, Char *felt* free in spite of, or because of, the precariousness all around. He felt free because he refused unfreedom in action.

"At every meal we eat together," Char said, "freedom is invited to sit down. The chair remains vacant, but the place is set."[5] Indeed, they set a place for freedom by taking three small but mighty steps: naming the unfreedom that was maiming and killing them; conjuring with their imaginations a more just and humane world up ahead, a world that could be or should be, but was not yet; and standing up collectively as destroyers of the old, and, therefore, harbingers of the new. Abolitionists. They would make themselves into new women and new men—the necessary creators of a new society.

———————

The specter of freedom can appear in contexts that are either decidedly nonviolent or overtly violent, indicating that the bright line between violence and nonviolence is in fact a wobbly line, largely mythological. Whenever the words "violence" or "nonviolence" land in the mouths of the powerful—any member of the ruling class, the 1 percent, or the chattering political class—beware their insincerity, their virtue-signaling, their deception and naked hypocrisy.

There was a time, not so long ago, when slavery was the normal and legal state of things. When Nat Turner or Gabriel Prosser or Denmark Vesey or hundreds of other freedom fighters led uprisings for freedom, they were immediately labeled violent savages. To *not* notice the crushing violence inherent to and congealed within the slave/master relationship is myopic at best; to see the slaves suddenly rise up, and to call that out—with righteous indignation—as violence is willful blindness. Remember Harriet Tubman with that explosive pistol in her pocket.

I recently met in an Illinois state prison a street-level drug dealer from Chicago who got into a beef with a rival, pulled a gun, and stole some money from him and is now doing ten years—a violent crime, no doubt about it. But I couldn't help thinking about the notorious Sackler family, billionaire owners of Purdue Pharma, who created the opioid crisis by knowingly unleashing and promoting the drug OxyContin, killing close to half a million people and destroying thousands of communities. Purdue Pharma pled guilty and forfeited $225 million— chump change for them, and there were no criminal charges against the Sacklers. Why? Because they're all "nonviolent" lawbreakers. I also wondered how that drug dealer might have fared if he'd had a million-dollar legal defense team.

The "good people" are all nonviolent, we're told by the overlords (without a hint of irony) because violence is ineffective, counterproductive, and always unacceptable. Violence is immoral. But look a little closer at the people trumpeting those echoing slogans—the prosperous and the powerful—and note that they are oozing false virtue, throwing sand in everyone's eyes, dripping with blood and hiding the evidence, all of them. It was the LAPD who initiated the attack on the Panther office, but, according to the police spokesman, that's because the Panthers were violent; the Chicago police drugged and then assassinated Panther leader Fred Hampton in his bed in 1970, but the police were portrayed for years as acting in self-defense. If they really believed that violence was ineffective, unacceptable, and immoral, then they wouldn't have murdered Fred Hampton, wouldn't have assassinated Patrice Lumumba or overthrown the elected government of Chile or invaded and occupied Vietnam, wouldn't be armed to the teeth themselves, unleashing their legions everywhere in the world, creating a militarized, carceral state at home, and nourishing a hyperaggressive war culture. No, their opposition to "violence" is super-selective—"We can be as violent as we please, but the rest of you must stand down." More honestly, they could simply say that they want a monopoly on violence for themselves, obedience and compliance from everyone else. Violence is, as H. Rap Brown from SNCC famously said decades ago, as American as cherry pie.

Nonviolence to the powerful means nothing more than passivity, conformity, and acquiescence. When they say "Be nonviolent," they are not encouraging fierce labor stoppages or militant direct actions. They are not saluting the militants of Extinction Rebellion, Earth First!, or United Nurses, nor the Palestinian strategy of Boycott, Divestment, and Sanctions—all nonviolent initiatives. No, they mean "Sit down and shut up."

More than fifty years ago, Martin Luther King Jr., refusing to condemn participants in the Watts rebellion, called the US government "the greatest purveyor of violence on earth."[6] He was right, of course, and that judgment holds true: the US not only ranks number one in military spending worldwide; it's also the number-one global arms dealer, a super-spreader of high-tech killing machines, as well as handguns and low-end murderous weapons.

But bullets and bombs aren't the only ways to kill people. Bad hospitals and a predatory health-care system also kill people. Government-sponsored enclosures—ghettos—also kill people. Forgotten communities and collapsing buildings kill people. Decomposing schools and brainwashing curriculums kill people. The unhoused have a life expectancy thirty years less than the general population. Thirty years! Violent deaths, quietly executed.

The nonviolence of peace and freedom activists like Martin Luther King Jr., Dorothy Day, David Dellinger, or Thich Nhat Hanh was not passive but, rather, aggressive and defiant. Their nonviolence confronted and exposed illegitimate state violence with the moral right of the people to be treated as fully human. And, of course, in the US South, many of the freedom organizers and civil rights workers by day were protected by armed local community people by night. SNCC leader Charlie Cobb wrote a smart and beautiful book about this contradiction appropriately called *This Nonviolent Stuff'll Get You Killed: How Guns Made the Civil Rights Movement Possible*.

Nonviolence can be a brilliant and creative tactic in the hands of the oppressed, and violence is indeed abhorrent, but these categories are neither neat nor fixed.

In our given world, the world as such, we're challenged to set a place at the table for freedom. We open our eyes wide, shake ourselves awake, and look closely at our real conditions: the beauty, the joy, and the ecstasy in every direction, as well as the undeserved pain and the unnecessary suffering. We open a space for freedom—we set a place at the table—when we identify the *unfreedoms* pressing us down and endangering our lives and our human dignity, imagine a better world for all, and act to resist and someday *abolish* unfreedom.

The overlapping and escalating crises we face today—the sum of our unfreedoms—can, of course, be seen and experienced as overwhelming, but we must somehow name and untangle them if we're to set a place for freedom to sit. Frederick Douglass identified slavery as cruel and inhuman. His words, uttered in Rochester, New York, on July 4, 1852, still resonate:

> What, to the American slave, is your Fourth of July? I answer: a day that reveals to him, more than all other days of the year, the gross injustice and cruelty to which he is a constant victim. To him, your celebration is a sham; your boasted liberty, an unholy license; your national greatness, swelling vanity; your sounds of rejoicing are empty and heartless; your denunciation of tyrants, brass fronted impudence; your shouts of liberty and equality, hollow mockery; your prayers and hymns, your sermons and thanksgivings, with all your religious parade and solemnity, are, to Him, mere bombast, fraud, deception, impiety, and hypocrisy—a thin veil to cover up crimes that would disgrace a nation of savages. There is not a nation of the earth guilty of practices more shocking and bloody than are the people of these United States at this very hour.[7]

Rene Char later named and fought the Nazi occupation; William Pharr identified and resisted LAPD occupation and brutality. We can start by naming the voracious greed of imperialism that subjugates nations and thrives on white supremacy, creating a parasitic economy in the elite center while impoverishing Black and Brown communities, and pillaging Third World countries. And we can name cataclysmic capitalist climate collapse—raging hurricanes, melting ice caps, rising oceans, angry wildfires and deforestation, the shredding of the earth's protective shield, the accelerating extermination and disappearance of creatures from fish and birds and insects to tigers and chimpanzees and Asian elephants—driven by unchecked extraction, reckless acquisitiveness, and the everyday operations of predatory racial capitalism that threaten to extinguish the possibility of sustained human life on earth. Unfreedom.

We can name the unfreedom of empire, unapologetically resurrected now in a cauldron of deliberately constructed fear, and under the
banner of renewed patriotic nationalism signaling an era of continuous
war and unprecedented military expansion: US troops based in hundreds of countries, an annual "national security" budget two-and-a-half
times that of China, and more than the national security budgets of
the next nine countries, including China and Russia, combined. We
live in a world where $2 *trillion* is spent annually on weapons of mass
murder (half of it spent by the US alone), compared to the $3 billion
allotted for the entire United Nation's annual budget. We live in a state
of US-sponsored permanent war, at home and abroad, with militarized
police forces acting as aggressive occupying armies in working-class
communities, and the never-ending serial shootings and killings of
Black citizens accompanied by a war culture that glorifies violence
and rewards obedience. And, of course, war and war culture generate
a vast empire of bullshit—in times of war the truth cannot keep up.
Unfreedom.

And we can name the ongoing crises created by the legacy of white
supremacy, settler colonialism, land theft, slavery and its long, shadowy
afterlife: a vast incarceration nation with over two million of our fellow
citizens—overwhelmingly Black and Brown people—living in cages and
subject to the most cruel and dehumanizing treatment by state agents,
and over four million more under some form of state supervision. With
under 5 percent of the world's population, the US holds 29 percent of
the world's prisoners.[8] The gulag stretches the length and breadth of
the country, with mass incarceration now a defining characteristic in
the "land of the free" and white supremacy reigning triumphant in
the "home of the brave." Superficial acknowledgment of a "troubling
past" accompanied by cosmetic reforms aimed at ameliorating protest
and rebellion—it's actually wonderful that we suddenly have a federal
holiday celebrating Juneteenth and an acknowledgment of the last
enslaved workers to learn of the Emancipation Proclamation, but don't
forget that it was hurriedly passed while a mass movement for justice
was mobilizing in the streets—will not be sufficient as long as white
supremacy as a system (in health disparities, wage gaps, life chances,

segregation in schools and housing and criminal justice, for example) grinds on, and growing calls for reparations for stolen land and labor are ignored or kicked to the curb by power. Another unfreedom.

We name the organized reactionary-led attack on women's liberation that has won several major victories, including a decision by the most powerful court in the country that denies all women bodily integrity and declares that the state has an absolute right to a woman's body, up to and including the right to require a pregnant woman to give birth and, in other circumstances, to take a baby from its mother. Note that our country went through a dark season not so long ago when the eugenics theory of racial purity was in vogue, and women were sterilized without their consent, and we endured an even longer period when some women were required by the state to give birth, even (or specifically) in cases of rape—the days of chattel slavery. That was also a period of seizing babies from their mothers, a time of zero reproductive freedom for some women. Oh and then, after claiming the body, the state faces no responsibility to feed, shelter, clothe, or in any other way take care of the body in custody. Unfreedom.

Racial capitalism is always in crisis (that's a feature, not a bug), and it is inherently predatory (not a flaw but a characteristic). The system has overdeveloped the selfish instinct in each of us and underdeveloped a natural countervailing capacity: the ability to embrace one another fully as equals. Our culture of extreme selfishness obliterates any clarity concerning the necessary dialectic between individual and community, between "me" and "we." Fueled by the distinctly American illusion of the Rugged Individual, self-absorption is normalized, greed is customary, intense self-regard and total blindness to others is expected, and egomaniacal actions are rewarded. In Bertolt Brecht's iconic poem "A Worker Reads History," he asks who built the seven gates of Thebes: Was it the kings who hauled the craggy blocks of stone?[9]

The US juggernaut is headed for catastrophe, either a new and sophisticated form of friendly-looking and familiar fascism, or some other form of extreme social disintegration. Another world is surely coming—greater equality, socialism, participatory democracy, and peace are all within our reach, but complete environmental collapse, nuclear war, work camps, and slavery are also possibilities. There are choices and options, and nothing is certain. Where do we go from here? A season of light or a season of darkness? Chaos or community? Barbarism or socialism?

Unfreedom can give us a snapshot of what is, and a powerful glimpse of what could be—the things we need to see clearly in order to resist effectively—but it is in no way a picture of inevitability. To think more deeply about what we're fighting for, we can deploy two overlapping plans of action: we nourish and unleash our wildest imaginations, and we search simultaneously for the seeds of the new growing inside the dying shell of the old—what the contemporary freedom fighter Mariame Kaba has called the "one million experiments" of resistance and world-building to be found in every crack and corner of the country and the planet.[10]

Frederick Douglass, Rene Char, and William Pharr understood their predicaments, but they must have seen something else as well—something shimmering on the far horizons of their minds, something that beckoned them to transcend the status quo that had been presented to them as inevitable and immutable. An image awakened inside each of them, and a voice said clearly, "The way things are is not the way things have to be, nor the way things will be forever." With that voice echoing and the dream forming in their minds, they rose up and surpassed the treacherous situations that were thrust upon them. Their imaginations unleashed a deeper humanity. Each was a freedom fighter, to be sure, but each was also a dreamer.

We're sometimes accused by friends and comrades of being idealists, romantics, utopians. Guilty! We're idealists in the sense of having ideals we're willing to work toward, but we are neither naive nor credulous. We're utopian in the sense of wanting to generate a dynamic vision of the possible, but not in some gauzy belief in the Garden of Eden, nirvana, heaven—images of innocent joy and pure delight, free of worry or pain or suffering or conflict or struggle or death, free, in fact, of the core elements of the human condition. We look to the Uruguayan writer Eduardo Galeano, who, when asked what good Utopia was, replied, "It's true. If I walk two steps toward Utopia, Utopia walks two steps away. If I walk ten steps toward Utopia, it walks ten steps away. So what good is Utopia?" His answer: "It's good for walking."[11] Yes, let's keep walking; let's keep dreaming; let's keep participating however we can in those one million experiments; let's keep doing what needs to be done, again and again.

Every human being is endowed with the powerful and unique capacity to imagine—it's the primary weapon of the weak. Maxine Greene reminds those of us who believe in freedom to make a distinction between castles in the sky and a tougher, more focused imagination; she calls it a *social imagination*. She points out that it took an imagination to conjure up Auschwitz, and that we should beware of a solitary imagination disconnected from a collective project of enlightenment and liberation. We want to nourish a common imagination in combat with our aggregated subjugation.

In a battle between the ruling class's army and our army, we will lose mightily, every time. But in a struggle between our moral vision—our social imaginations—and theirs, we can win. And we must. So let's set the battle on our own terms, an engagement of the imaginaries, a guerrilla action of the dreamers, a war of the flea, poking and jabbing against the hulking, mechanized, and monstrous invading army.

We can experience difficulty nourishing our imaginations, and we can stumble over envisioning another society with a different set of social relations that could and should be organized to our common advantage. It's well known that we find it easier to imagine the end of the world—after all, we've seen it on TV and at the movies, repeatedly—than to imagine the end of prisons or the end of police or the end of capitalism. We need to push our imaginative horizons, develop and deploy a new language that is freed from the bleak, unimaginative frames on offer: free markets versus state control. Albert Einstein famously noted, "Imagination is more important than knowledge. Knowledge is limited. Imagination encircles the world."[12] Liberation and enlightenment are products of the arts—and of the imagination.

The capacity to see the world as if it could be otherwise creates yearning and liberates desire; we are freed (or condemned) to run riot. Art—subversive, unruly, and disruptive—can inspire the upheaval, challenging the status quo simply by opening us to consider the alternatives; suddenly the taken-for-granted and the given world become unbearable. Emily Dickinson proposed that the imagination can light the slow fuse of possibility.[13] Our work includes reaching for the candle, striking the match, and lighting that fuse.

3

"LADY FREEDOM AMONG US"

"LADY FREEDOM AMONG US"

*don't lower your eyes
or stare straight ahead to where
you think you ought to be going*

*don't mutter oh no
not another one
get a job fly a kite
go bury a bone*

*with her oldfashioned sandals
with her leaden skirts
with her stained cheeks and whiskers and heaped up trinkets
she has risen among us in blunt reproach*

*she has fitted her hair under a hand-me-down cap
and spruced it up with feathers and stars
slung over her shoulder she bears
the rainbowed layers of charity and murmurs
all of you even the least of you*

*don't cross to the other side of the square
don't think another item to fit on a tourist's agenda*

*consider her drenched gaze her shining brow
she who has brought mercy back into the streets
and will not retire politely to the potter's field*

*having assumed the thick skin of this town
its gritted exhaust its sunscorch and blear
she rests in her weathered plumage
bigboned resolute*

*don't think you can forget her
don't even try
she's not going to budge*

no choice but to grant her space
crown her with sky
for she is one of the many
and she is each of us

—RITA DOVE

> R eflecting on your ethical tradition, or the moral framework you've developed for yourself and that you try to embody in your everyday life, what is your responsibility to a proximate stranger in distress?

— REFLECTION THREE: SOCIAL FREEDOM/INDIVIDUAL LIBERTY —

The dazzling poet Rita Dove, Pulitzer Prize winner and former US poet laureate, was visiting Battery Park, where tourists gather every day for picnics and bike rides and ferry excursions to the Statue of Liberty. The statue, a gift from France meant to celebrate the abolition of slavery, resides in the middle of New York harbor, standing tall with her torch held high, and with the words of the socialist poet Emma Lazarus's "The New Colossus" inscribed:

> Not like the brazen giant of Greek fame, / With conquering limbs astride from land to land; / Here at our sea-washed, sunset gates shall stand / A mighty woman with a torch, whose flame / Is the imprisoned lightning, and her name / Mother of Exiles. From her beacon-hand / Glows world-wide welcome; her mild eyes command / The air-bridged harbor that twin cities frame. / "Keep, ancient lands, your storied pomp!" cries she / With silent lips. "Give me your tired, your poor, / Your huddled masses yearning to breathe free, / The wretched refuse of your teeming shore. / Send these, the homeless, tempest-tost to me, / I lift my lamp beside the golden door!"[1]

You may not be aware that the poet named the statue the "Mother of Exiles," but every American schoolchild learned those last few lines;

Rita Dove knew the whole poem, as well as the poet's socialist-activist legacy. The mighty statue was encased in scaffolding and in the process of being restored on the day of Rita Dove's visit, but right in front of the poet, unobscured and clear as day, sat a homeless woman, "big boned" and "resolute." Rita Dove doesn't miss the dazzling symmetry or the aching conflict—echoes and reverberations, traces and shadows inform every line.

The poet effectively reworks Emma Lazarus's lofty inscription into a powerful reflection on the contradiction: the Mother of Exiles, that mighty woman lifting the torch of freedom, welcoming the immigrant, the asylum seeker, and the homeless masses yearning to breathe free, is ridiculed by the presence of that other woman, "Lady Freedom among us," who is unhoused, unfed, and unfree. The unhoused woman in front of our eyes makes a mockery of the statue's aspirational legend.

The subject of Rita Dove's poem with her "old fashioned sandals" and her "leaden skirts" is "one of the many and she is each of us." Here the poet illuminates a fundamental contradiction at the heart of our examination of the dense and layered concept of freedom as well as at the center of the human condition: we are each fully the one of one—full stop; we are each merely one of the many—again, full stop.

F reedom struggles and social justice movements throughout history (and to this day) have fought for individual liberties—the right to vote, to access public goods and resources, to speak one's truth, to participate in the full life of society, to receive equal pay for equal work, to live and eat and sit and drink water where one wished—always embedded within a larger vision of collective freedom for an entire community or a whole people. "Black liberation," "women's liberation," "disability rights," "worker's rights," "gay liberation"—each movement brought a community into being through the process of first naming themselves, designating the oppression, discrimination, ill-treatment, or abuse one faced based on membership in that specific group and then rising up to fight back. In the act of collectively naming themselves in resistance to a common oppression, individuals forged themselves into a community and created an identifiable *public.*

Barriers to freedom and liberation arise on the level of personal liberty and on the level of collective freedom; the resistance exists on both levels, and the test of success can be measured on each level as well. But it's easy in America to default to the individual—*my* rights and *my* freedom—and to ignore or remain ignorant of the commons.

To take one central and electrifying example, the US—its wealth and power, its culture and customs, its laws and government—was built on an elaborate architecture of white supremacy that includes the system of slavery and the practice of conquest, war, and genocide, the defeat of Reconstruction, and more. Everyday bigotry and racist ideas bloom in the nourishing shade of those structures of inequality based on color. For many well-intentioned liberals, the path to repairing past harms is to be found exclusively in individuals, one by one, "unlearning racism" or embracing "diversity, equity, and inclusion." The definition of the problem leads to a specific theory of action: if the problem is merely a bad idea inside some people's heads, the solution is in psychology and persuasion. But if instead the problem is structural, then action must involve dismantling those structures. "Unlearning racism" is a doomed project precisely because a collective catastrophe—vast structural inequities never repaired, centuries of exploitation and oppression and generational trauma caused by our laws and backed by armed agents of the state—demands a collective response. The harm was instituted by the government and embraced by the dominant society; any authentic repair must be social and shared as well, borne by the collective, and also at the highest levels. Reparations would include, then, institutional transformations and structural rearrangement in every area of social life. Individual attitudes matter, but they cannot drive that kind of repair.

The word "racism" can implicate a singular person or the collective, and in our hyper-individualistic culture, the word most commonly devolves to a singular individual who did something obviously prejudiced: "He's a racist"; "She's being racist"; "I'm not a racist." It's about this or that person or particular act or behavior, and it means "bigoted, backward, stupid, and offensive." People like Cliven Bundy, a Nevada cattle rancher who staged an armed standoff with the federal government over grazing rights and said in an interview in 2014 that African Americans were better off under slavery, is clearly making a racist statement.[2] Amy Cooper, too, was acting on a racist assumption in 2020 when she called 911 because a bird-watcher asked her to keep her dog on a leash; she famously said, "There is an African American man . . . threatening myself and my dog. Please, send the cops immediately!" But since *I'm* not backward and bigoted and stupid like them, "I'm not racist."[3] Convenient for white liberals, but not helpful in repairing the real harm.

We live in a society—a collective social order—built upon white supremacy through law and custom, history and culture. Our collective life is structured on perpetuating racial oppression. So, wherever and whoever you are, you can close your eyes to reality and simply go along, or you can keep an eye on policy or law, you can do the work of searching out, opposing, and dismantling the institutional and structural expressions of white supremacy, privilege and oppression based on color, which is structural racism.

Health disparities, criminal legal exposure, educational access, housing imbalances—all of these arrangements and frameworks express a white supremacist reality. You don't say the N-word? Good for you. You're still living in a racist society and breathing the toxic fumes of racial oppression. Any whole-hearted anti-racist response must include struggling against those sturdy, embedded frames of white supremacy.

The wellspring of bigotry and racial prejudice is, after all, the structure of inequality itself, not the other way around. That is, the reality of inequality baked into law and economic condition as well as history, custom, and culture generates racist thoughts and feelings as justification. Those racist ideas keep regenerating as long as the structures of white supremacy and Black oppression are in place. Race itself is, of course, both everywhere and nowhere—a social construction, a massive fiction, and, at the same time, the hardest of hard-edged realities.

The simplistic reduction to the individual not only allows people to dodge any social responsibility whatsoever themselves, but it also blinds us to the egregious activities of Donald Sterling, for example, who became rich and powerful as a real estate magnate dealing in segregated and slum housing, but only got called out as racist and lost his NBA franchise when he disparaged African Americans in a taped phone call made public. Slumlording didn't warrant any sanction whatsoever. The list goes on: a Chicago mayor shuttered more than fifty public schools in predominantly Black communities while he militarized a bloated and aggressive police force, covered up police murders in Black communities, but never used the N-word, so, "not a racist"; a slick and charming president pushed harsh legislation that resulted in escalating incarceration and the overrepresentation of Black people in prisons but loved Black music, so, "not racist." But each of these cases—and zillions more—are examples of white supremacy and racist structures in practice and social reality.

I am the one and only human being just like me who ever walked this earth, and the only one who ever was or ever will be just like me—there can be no other. And the same is true of you. We are induplicable. So when I die or when you die, the world will go on without us, and at the same time a singular universe will collapse, and all the webs of significance I've strung between the films I've seen and the books I've read, all the places I've been, the people I've loved, the incidents and episodes I've experienced, and all the knowledge I've gathered, will vanish in a flash. The unique interaction of emotions, desires, loves, insights, perceptions, practices, thoughts and feelings that are mine and mine alone—my hikes in the city, long swims in the lake and the ocean, shooting through the rapids, making love, walking the Inca Trail, fighting the police, going to jail, biking in Beijing and Hong Kong and Chicago and along the Pacific Coast Highway, attending concerts, experimenting with this and that, going to classes, reading Oluale Kossola and Black Elk and Toni Morrison, listening to John Coltrane and Pharoh Sanders and Nina Simone and Bob Dylan, working in the shipyards, seizing (and wasting) my time, becoming a merchant sailor, stopping traffic, disrupting army recruiters, organizing a community union, engaging with comrades, talking with strangers, studying revolution, practicing my everyday anarchist calisthenics, raising three kids, teaching preschool as well as graduate school, eating on the streets of Hanoi, making bread, taking grandchildren to the parks and the museums, racing in a panic to the ER—all of it will black out and disappear with me. Even though I always knew this was true (stars are exploding all around us, worlds are disintegrating, and those not busy being born are surely busy dying), it's all still a bit sad for me to think about that vast and seemingly endless landscape erased. Again, the same is true of you, all of you—as Rita Dove says, even the least of you.

I am at the same time, like the proximate stranger in Rita Dove's poem, simply one of the many, exactly like you (and all others) in so many important ways. I was born; if I'm cut, I bleed; and someday I will die. I'm a human being, and I share a human culture and a human fate with all other human beings; we share, as well, these specific few moments in time. Just like Dove's Lady Freedom ("she is one of the many / and she is each of us") just like you. What doesn't die, what's not snuffed out, is the social organism—the ongoing community and culture—that we build and rebuild in every generation—if, and how, we choose.

My friend Lisa Lee, a passionate student of Theodor Adorno, argues alongside him that we become free human beings only when we go outside of ourselves and enter into relationship with others. It's impossible to be free as an isolated individual; we are only free when we acknowledge ourselves in others, and others in ourselves. When we hand ourselves over to others, we achieve our freedom in community.

———

Herman Melville's novella *Benito Cereno* tells the story of a New England sealing ship operating off the coast of Chile in 1805 that comes upon a Spanish frigate drifting aimlessly with tattered sails, a distressed crew, and a figurehead oddly shrouded in canvas bearing the painted slogan "Follow Your Leader." A small party led by Captain Amasa Delano boards the ship to assess the situation and assist if possible. There they encounter a skeleton crew and a diminished cargo of enslaved people as well as Captain Benito Cereno, who explains the troubles that had brought them to this point: terrible storms, he claims, ill fate and bad luck, disease and fevers that had taken the lives of several, including the slave master Alexandro Aranda.[4]

Captain Delano spends hours aboard the ship talking with Benito Cereno, who is always in the company of his loyal enslaved servant, Babo. Delano notes a series of strange events: urgent whispering among crew and cargo, a few Africans carrying knives, and an occasional physical confrontation with Spanish crew members. Benito Cereno is pale and weak, often near fainting, always insisting that Babo stay close. As Delano prepares to return to his own ship, a desperate Benito Cereno leaps from the deck onto the departing long boat and the truth becomes clear: Babo is running the ship and Benito Cereno is his prisoner; insurgent rebels have freed themselves, taken control of the ship, and are demanding a return to Africa; the shrouded figurehead is the bones of Alexandro Aranda, the painted slogan a targeted threat to the crew.

The entire day had been a complex dramatic performance put on by the Africans under the directorial brilliance of Babo to deceive the visitors. But in order to see the reality of the drama produced on his behalf—which is bursting with hints and clues and full-blown illumination—Captain Delano, a good liberal Republican from New England, would have needed the one quality he lacked: a sincere belief that Babo and the other enslaved cargo were full human beings like himself, people capable of intricate planning, complex intelligence, wild imagination, and historical memory, as well as an acute sense of their own agency. Delano couldn't see it because to see it he would have had to escape the anesthetizing effect of his blinding privilege and assumed not that Babo was less than human, but that Babo was exactly as human as himself: the one of one, and one of the many. Privilege, that easily available and highly addictive hard drug (widely available today), had anesthetized them and knocked them out—they were sleeping the deep, deep American sleep.

When I was first teaching at the University of Illinois at Chicago, a large urban campus in the heart of the city, my classes all met at night to accommodate adult students who worked. I was there for several months before I began to notice that the male students (and I) quickly scattered for home after class, while the women students seemed to gather together in order to go as a group to the parking lot or the train. When I asked one woman about it, she smiled a kind of pitying smile and said that yes, it was true, of course—the women were banding together for safety. She practically said, "Duh!" and I was embarrassed. Male privilege allowed me, and encouraged all of us men, not to notice. We coordinated our after-class routine from then on, and we learned a lesson: effectively wrestling with privilege is not about grappling with guilt or shame. It's about contending with a deadly addictive drug that you didn't necessarily ask for, embrace or even recognize, but that is on offer for free, and that will, once you become an addict, drive you blind. Resisting privilege is a portal opening toward a larger humanity.

Benito Cereno illuminates a vibrant world that white people—sightless and sleep-walking—could not begin to perceive through the dark cloud of slavery and its evil spawn, the ideology of white supremacy. Because they could not see themselves in Babo and his comrades, because they could not see Babo in them, they were both sightless and mindless: blind people who thought they could see, seeing people who were in fact blind. Reality eluded them, and they could not be free. This is our continuing challenge.

In his 1968 hit song "Everyday People," Sylvester Stewart, better known with his group Sly and the Family Stone, says: "I am no better, and neither are you / We are the same whatever we do."[5] Yes, yes, there we are, each and all of us: singular everyday people. And we'd do better if we saw one another—deeply, truly, fully.

Holding on to the truth embodied in the contradiction is a struggle, and naming the challenge can help: I automatically see the world through my own narcissistic eyes—my eyes, after all, are the only eyes I've got—and yet I have a mind that tells me that my entire being depends on the love and the care and the labor of others, both historically and right now. Food, water, shelter, work, sanitation—there's a vast collective propping me up and keeping me alive. But if I get too "Kumbaya, My Lord," and Sly Stone about it, I fall into an opposite trap: I homogenize humanity and miss the essential learning only to be found in our profound differences. "Common ground" can become counterproductive, even reactionary, if it normalizes dominance, dogma, or suffocating doctrine; we also need to embrace uncommon ground as a space of dynamic learning and the possibility of forward-looking change. A worthwhile practice is to notice the dialectic, followed by a helpful mantra to recite: all individuals are like no others; all individuals are like some others; all individuals are like all others.

The ancient Jewish sage Hillel the Elder, author of the "Golden Rule," famously asked, "If I'm not for myself, who will be? If I'm for myself alone, what am I?"[6] Those paired and penetrating questions have troubled and guided people in every age and society, every classroom or community—selfish/selfless, thoughtless/considerate, oneness/separateness, grasping/generous. Both/and. There is no easy resolution; we ride the contradiction, loving our own lives fully and honoring the lives of others fully—seeing them, hearing them, embracing them. Diving into the contradiction, surfing the maelstrom, has illuminated vast social, cultural, philosophical, and political spaces for millennia.

I can't be free unless we are free; we can't be free if you are not free. The dialectic—the tension—between individuals and society. We have a choice when it comes to freedom, and in stark terms, it's this: the freedom to exploit and destroy, the freedom of the market, or the freedom to live in harmony with one another by making provision for mutual security, including food and housing, income, healthcare, and education. This second choice would move beyond "freedom from" and toward "freedom with."

The contradiction broke down in the United States when the country's elite rejected any sense of community and lurched violently toward an exclusive "me" in politics and policies with the self-proclaimed "Reagan Revolution." This meant fierce opposition to any concept of collectivity or the "public," weaponized individualism, and a peculiarly anemic, libertarian definition of "freedom." "Public safety" became "own a gun"; "public education" became a product to be bought exclusively at the market place; "public health" was reduced to a commodity sold over the counter accompanied by a warning: "Take care of yourself, by yourself." The word "public" became a racist dog whistle in several contexts: public welfare was not a term hurled at corporate tax write-offs or Delaware tax shelters or so-called public/ private partnerships; public housing didn't refer to tax breaks for real estate developers; public aid never meant farm subsidies. The word "freedom" surrendered to the rising worship of the individual and became a bloodless husk: my freedom to sell flavored vaping products, or to graze my cattle in a national park, or to carry my assault weapon into the grocery store—the public be damned.

Ronald Reagan famously campaigned for the presidency defending "freedom" and "states' rights" at the Neshoba County Fair in Mississippi, a short distance from the lynching site of civil rights martyrs Andrew Goodman, James Chaney, and Micky Schwerner. He later said at his inauguration in 1981: "Government is not the solution to our problem. Government is the problem."[7] Britain's Margaret Thatcher provided an addendum to Reagan's proclamation in 1987: "Too many . . . have been given to understand 'I have a problem, it is the government's job to cope with it!' . . . They are casting their problems on society, and who is society? There is no such thing!"[8]

These ideological pillars—there is no society, and government is the problem—became fused into a single orthodoxy that came to be called neoliberalism: the "free" market rules everything, unencumbered by government programs that, no matter how well intended, only stifle or stall the market, the only true source of wisdom, and the engine of every sensible solution to people's needs. Each self-interested individual is "free," standing alone, unaided, and radically responsible for himself and his family (the "family" being the only legitimate arrangement of collective living), and anything that bends toward the communal or the collective must be sniffed out and destroyed. This helps explain the reduction or disappearance of checks on or regulatory action against corporate greed, as well as the sustained attacks on Social Security, Amtrak, and the US Postal Service—assaults that seem silly at times, but, in this larger ideological struggle, make a certain perverse sense.

Americans are renowned the world around for our individualism, and here we stand: no public health system, grinding labor and galloping poverty for the many and escalating opulence for the few, chronic insecurity, massive homelessness and hunger, the dramatic unraveling of social programs, the disappearance of public education, and the collapse of infrastructure, including city water systems. This state of affairs is justified with an anemic set of rationalizations: poor people made poor decisions or they wouldn't be poor; unhoused people should have paid their rent; unemployed people should get jobs; people with mental illnesses should cheer up and straighten up; people in prison did bad things and must live in cages, possibly forever. In short, the US can't look after its own people, so, buck up, trust God, and love capitalism—pretty much the same thing.

We're suspended in a cruel contradiction: our government is rich enough and powerful enough to conduct several wars simultaneously all over the world, but it cannot guarantee its people the most basic human rights like food or shelter, education or health care, without which freedom is a farce. The country calls itself a democracy but allows some people to hoard so much wealth that they effectively own and control the government; there are enough resources in the world to fulfil human needs, but not enough to fulfill capitalist greed.

This signature national trademark resembles what political scientist Norman Geras called "the contract of mutual indifference": a sense of doomed loneliness, of abandonment, a powerful realization that because I am not responsible for anyone else, I'm on my own if I should be faced with any difficulties.[9] "I won't help you when you're in distress," the featured ethic dictates. "And I guess—woe is me—that when I'm in need, you won't help me either." We are free, and we are entirely alone. Of course, it's completely human to be inconsistent, so, while you're on your own, when I need the ER, I expect it to be fully staffed and generously funded; every reactionary politician in Texas is a self-reliant lone star right up until the next hurricane hits and he cleverly transforms before your eyes into an enthusiastic member of the national collective.

This ideology didn't suddenly fall from the sky; it was years in the making, constructed on a powerful base, and held together with iron-tough props and sturdy struts that are baked deep into our American DNA. The rugged individual Indian-killer Davey Crockett, the Marlboro Man, John Wayne, and the frontiersman, the fabled humble origins of every politician who "succeeded" by his own wit and grit, the self-made man, the Lone Ranger—this is toxic individualism, weaponized and ready to rumble.

Our culture of extreme individualism has the familiar stench of common sense. It's sold to us as "human nature," and it has the effect of disarming people in the face of collective problems—a pandemic, for example, or catastrophic climate collapse. We're accustomed to hearing nonsensical statements like "Only you can prevent forest fires," and we nod dully instead of screaming, "What about climate change, the timber industry, forest maintenance policy, real estate developers given free rein to build residential tracts in fire (or flood) plains?" We heard a politician recently say in all seriousness that Tampa faces different environmental problems than Miami, and that each community should work to solve the climate crisis on its own. Good luck, Miami. And an item on the nightly news recently featured a chilling report about the dying ocean that included a long interview with a leader of a well-meaning liberal environmental group. When asked if there was anything individuals could do, she offered a long list of possibilities (eat lower on the food chain, recycle plastic) without pointing to any acts that would build collective opposition and power or address structural issues. Facing imminent destruction, our rich and powerful society seems willing to commit suicide rather than link arms and face reality collectively. In this landscape, freedom is always personal and individual, and anything social or shared is an infringement on *my freedom*. How lonely, how sad, and how blazingly self-destructive.

Extreme individualism locates problems and searches for solutions in the narrowest terms. Consider a familiar phenomenon in modern

American life: the unremarkable weight-loss diet. It's an individual issue, right? An issue as ordinary as mud. Look at the diet news coverage, the diet industry, or the national diet obsession and you'll see overwhelmingly the focus is on YOU or YOU, or on some other individual who wants or needs to lose weight. It's your problem or challenge or responsibility, and there is barely a nod in the direction of a social element. Fat people are lazy or undisciplined; serial dieters have a character flaw or a psychological problem. That's "common sense"—and there's nothing shriller and more insistent than common sense, especially when it's entirely wrong.

Big Food, like the tobacco and drug industries before it, has created an entire system—huge marketing budgets that target young people, fraudulent studies to confuse the impact of lethal products, massive PR campaigns to resist attempts to force them to take any responsibility whatsoever—designed to maximize profits while poisoning masses of people. "Shouldn't I be free to market a product people want?" they ask. Shouldn't people be free to buy the sodas and snacks of their choice? And, like the gambling industry, the house is stacked mercilessly against the individual. The food advertising budget is $14 billion a year—mostly pushing sugary drinks, fast food, candy and highly processed snacks—compared to less than $1 billion a year for the Centers for Disease Control and Prevention focused on "health promotion and chronic disease prevention."[10]

There are five fast-food restaurants for every supermarket in our country, and they're most likely found in poorer areas; 12 percent of Americans go hungry, and their options are often ultraprocessed food or no food at all; more than half of our total calories now come from ultraprocessed food, stripped of nutrients and filled with sugar, and the result is that *most* of us are overweight, and chronic diseases linked to diet are through the roof.[11] So, diet if you like, but, as Mark Bittman puts it, our real "weight problem" is the "dead weight of the profiteers who poison us and of the plutocrats who abet them."[12] All in the name of freedom.

Or consider the automobile, the ultimate symbol of freedom within the American dream. Imagine! Every individual tooling around in their massive steel unit, free to turn left or right, to speed or stop, grinding up the environment, glorying in the chaos. We might have put that massive industrial capacity, that brilliant engineering knowledge, that labor, and all that money into creating public transit: bullet trains for long distance, interlocking electric shuttles to every desired point. We could do that now. Instead, all the money and excitement go to—what?—self-driving cars and expanding Uber and Lyft. Another iteration of individualism in which each unit is attended by its own robot. A nightmare of anti-community and a disaster for the environment, but, in the individualist ideology, striking a blow for freedom.

In our collapsed culture we lean toward an exclusive me-ness and tend to talk about moral behavior and ethical action in individualistic terms, ignoring or eliminating any social dimension, although a collective element is always there. After all, most Spartans act like Spartans, most Athenians act like Athenians, and, for better and for worse, most Americans act like Americans. Almost everyone would agree that individuals should not lie, steal, or assault others. That's conventional—but being conventional and embodying personal virtues is not the same thing as being moral. Being a moral person in an immoral society takes courage, consciousness, and the will to act. Moreover, establishing a just society is the essential path toward creating the conditions that will allow people who are acting conventionally—just doing what's normal and expected—to also be acting ethically. Case in point: during the days of chattel slavery, going along with everyday life meant participating (explicitly or implicitly) in evil. Once slavery was abolished, doing everyday things no longer carried the stench of kidnapping, human trafficking, and forced labor.

Mark Twain wrote a lovely essay called "Free Speech Is for the Grave" in which he outlined the power of conventional thinking and behavior, the desire to be liked and accepted, and the seeming rudeness of speaking out. His killer example was, of course, slavery—every acquaintance he knew opposed it; none spoke out against it, or even about it because that might be discourteous and create discomfort; better to just go along and get along.[13]

Let's return to that difficult but necessary tension between "me" and "we." The story of your life starts in the same place every day and spools forward with a familiar ring and rhythm: you wake up, and there you are in your bed, facing the day, constructing an entire world through your own thinking as you get dressed. You're a good person (pretty much— well, most of the time), you work hard (OK, hard enough), and you're mostly trying to do your best. Mostly. You're hungry, and you head to the kitchen for toast and your coffee or tea or miso soup. Let's go!

Everyone does that. It's natural and entirely common.

You head to your little isolated box on wheels, start the car, and steer onto the roadway toward your job. Why so much traffic—commuters are such a pain! You're in a hurry for an important meeting, and there are only a few cars in the ride-share lane, so you pull over there and speed up. Suddenly a woman veers in front of you and she's alone in her car—what an asshole! This is for ride-shares! You blast your horn and give her the finger because she's terrible. Of course, it's hard to take into account that all those other people on the road have things to do that are important to them, and it's impossible to gauge the relative importance of each, or to know, for example, that the asshole who cut you off was on her way to the ER where her son had been taken an hour earlier after crashing his motorcycle into a tree. Not your problem!

Each of us necessarily and naturally thinks, sees, feels, and hears in a severely limited and tightly restricted range. We don't see or hear or think everything that can be seen or heard or thought. How could we? We'd go insane if it were otherwise, and, in fact, one of the charming qualities of tiny infants is that they inhabit (and are protected by) a veil of unconsciousness—in the first days, while their eyes may be wide open, all they can take in is shadow and light and blurry shapes; they're all but deaf and blind, and they only awaken slowly, bit by bit. Their awakening is delightful: they smile with recognition; later they parallel play with other toddlers; then they make friends; much later we participate in class and group activities, becoming more and more effective and decent social beings; we even fall in love. But our awakenings are always contingent and partial, and our range of seeing and thinking and feeling naturally restricted. We each take a sweeping unitary wholeness—the universe—select a microscopic speck (me), and tell our stories, day after day, from that tiny point of view. That speck (ME!) (YOU!) becomes hyperreal and is perceived (by me or by you) to be the center of the universe. The story is not only *about* me; it's also *for* me. I'm the star of the movie, author, director, and lead actor in my life, and what's good *for me* is, well, good; and what's bad *for me* is, of course, bad. Everyone else in my life—family, colleagues, proximate strangers, the crowd—is a supporting actor or a bit player. Or just some annoying background noise, like those commuters.

When I think about everyday egoism this way, it seems a miracle that we can reach even tentative agreements with one another about the shape and scale of things, let alone achieve solid common understandings, or even intimacy with a partner. There's a lot of talk today about how we all live in self- and socially-constructed silos—political, cultural, national—but the first and primary silo is that initial theater for one. When you step back a bit, you realize that we are all deeply unreliable narrators, authors of a string of myths and tall tales.

Narcissism is our default. Listen to the language: my car, my son, my partner. Think about a seminar you might have attended with me (I like to call it *my* class), your dazzling (or irrelevant or slightly nutty) teacher—the class was real, we attended the same seminar, and yet you and I had markedly different experiences of seminar. If I said to my partner, "Seminar was great this morning," and you said to a friend, "Class was so boring that I kept nodding off," who's right?

Or, for example, a brief story about my birth family, narrated by me: My mom was a Pollyanna, my dad a workaholic, one of my brothers was out of touch with his feelings, another drank too much, and . . . I'll stop there. Note who is narrating this family story; note how impossible it is to imagine that my brother would tell the story this way: "Hi, I'm Bill's brother, my name's not important, and I'm quite out of touch with my feelings, but deeply impressed by Bill's insights, perceptions, and judgments." Unthinkable. And we all do this all the time: this colleague is boring, that friend takes up too much space, my next-door neighbor is a know-it-all. Judgments, judgments, judgments, always according to me, the central character in the carnival of my life.

So, we ought to note the massive rift between the world as it is and the world as each one of us thinks it is—mistaking our self-constructed little world for the whole wide world. And there is a potentially serious downside: if you believe emphatically enough that the world of your construction is in fact the whole wide world, filled with a lot of "ass-holes," and not a "construction" at all, then the we/me dialectic disappears, and you're drowning in selfishness. If you're willing to act with full force upon that misperception, arrogance and self-righteousness, bossiness and obnoxiousness, authoritarianism, autocracy, fascism, and more are sure to follow.

The writer George Saunders, arguing persuasively for the power of fiction and literature to rescue us from our myopic obsessions, asks us to think for a minute about Chicago, his and my hometown.[14] What comes immediately to mind? Lake Michigan? Wrigley Field? Deep-dish pizza? The Second City actors? Or the grid as you fly above the city landing at Midway? Perhaps Al Capone once upon a time, maybe Barack Obama or Oprah Winfrey now. You're missing a lot, naturally. But say you had for a moment the magic powers to take in all of Chicago, to swallow it whole—every smell and taste and alley and closet and cafe conversation and dresser drawer and shop and factory and pet and person and perspective. As soon as you did that, it would shift and time would move on, and the Chicago you magically grasped a moment ago would be gone. So what? Well, it's not a big problem, I guess, until one of my out-of-town friends says to me, "Chicago—wow! What should be done about Chicago?" Now I'm supposed to judge Chicago—guns, gangs, homelessness, failing schools, whatever stereotype or generalization is on offer at the moment—and do something about it. But the Chicago I or my friend or the mayor or the city council understand or imagine it to be is a shadowy palimpsest next to the pulsing, chaotic, throbbing, tumultuous, bubbling bedlam that is the real city on the lake.

And yet this is too often what we do with one another and with other people (those we know well, like family, as well as the proximate strangers we see on the street): we deploy our anemic projections, and then we enact our too-certain judgments. It's a problem, because that delusional gulf between the world as it is and the world as we construct it rears its weird and sometimes nasty head, and with it the return of arrogance and self-righteousness, bossiness and obnoxiousness, bullying, authoritarianism, and all the rest.

This aporia, the conflict, is ultimately unresolved and unresolvable, but you can read lots of imaginative literatures, putting yourself in the shoes of others, as George Saunders advises, or at least acknowledge the trap—and then leap fully into the contradiction, struggling to stay awake and aware, with your head above the rising water.

*

In Boots Riley's dazzling 2018 film *Sorry to Bother You*, a corporation called "Worry Free" promises customers free food and housing, and freedom from the stress of paying bills.[15] Wow!—no rent, no balancing budgets, no calculating taxes. Sounds terrific! People are rushing to sign up. But there's a catch: "Worry Free" requires participants to sign a lifetime work contract, and, before long, happy contractors are reduced to miserable beasts of burden—literally. Boots Riley's vivid imagination conjures up a modern-day system of slavery cleverly marketed to folks bathed in the blood of toxic individualism and our pervasive consumer culture. Slavery in this case comes wearing the congenial mask of freedom. And suddenly you wonder, Am I free, or how free am I, really? Do I have a kind of lifetime contract that says, in effect, work or starve?

Remember that freedom was the banner of the Union forces during the Civil War fighting to end the "peculiar institution" and free a people, but it was also the motto of the Confederacy—those organized traitors willing to burn down the whole house in pursuit of a single, exalted "freedom": their freedom to own other human beings. The freedom of 1776 was purchased by theft and captivity. And it's noteworthy that "freedom" is the cry of every carbon extractor, exploiter, invader, occupier, and sweatshop operator today. So, while the Confederacy was willing to destroy the nation for the proclaimed right to own people, the capitalist class has always lived off a system of wage slavery. They're now willing to destroy the ability of human beings and millions of other species to survive on Earth for their supposed freedom to exploit resources and people, hoarding their extravagant, ever-multiplying super-profits. All *me*, and never *we*.

What to do? We can start by applying the sensibilities of art to the way we live. We have imaginations that we can nurture, experiences we can map out and engage, and we have the capacity to wonder, reflect, discuss, debate, reach out, and keep on reaching. We can remind ourselves that we are but one of the many, and that every other ones-of-the-many is a vast universe in itself; if you follow any human being into their lived life for two minutes all categorical assumptions evaporate, and all one-dimensional stereotypes collapse. We can challenge ourselves to learn to live with empathy, ambiguity, doubt, skepticism, agnosticism, and uncertainty—always willing to question, and question, and then question some more. Always seeking to see ourselves in others, and others in ourselves, always nourishing a little humility.

The contradiction of life as it's lived, the unity of humanity, of everyone and everything is that you are an individual, of course, but that doesn't automatically enlist you as a soldier in the ideological cause of bitter, one-sided individualism. That's a choice. We can reject individualism in its poisonous form—romanticized, codified, and always at bottom an exercise in *selective* humanization. We can think of freedom in its collective/social shape and frame. We can choose to embrace humanity whole, to accept the rackety ruckus, to ride the wild, unruly tempest in the direction of our common and collective freedom dreams.

4

NO GODS, NO MASTERS

As we go marching, marching
In the beauty of the day
A million darkened kitchens
A thousand mill lofts gray
Are touched with all the radiance
That a sudden sun discloses
For the people hear us singing
Bread and roses, bread and roses

As we go marching, marching
We battle too for men
For they are women's children
And we mother them again
Our lives shall not be sweated
From birth until life closes
Hearts starve as well as bodies
Give us bread, but give us roses

As we go marching, marching
Unnumbered women dead
Go crying through our singing
Their ancient call for bread
Small art and love and beauty
Their drudging spirits knew
Yes, it is bread we fight for
But we fight for roses too

As we go marching, marching
We bring the greater days
For the rising of the women
Means the rising of the race
No more the drudge and idler
Tender toil where one reposes
But the sharing of lives glories
Bread and roses, bread and roses

—JAMES OPPENHEIM

Make four lists, side by side: first a list of the things you need to speak up about, things you ought to say out loud and into the world more often and more forcefully; next, make an inventory of chains (material or metaphoric, physical and psychological, social or cultural) holding you back from speaking up or acting out about what the known demands of you; then catalogue as best you can all the love that's in your heart; and finally, make a register of the thick iron bars and coils of barbed wire that keep us apart. Now write one page that summarizes how you're longing to live.

— **REFLECTION FOUR:** FREEDOM, ANARCHISM, AND SOCIALISM —

In 2011 I spent an exhilarating day with the legendary freedom fighter Manolis Glezos (1922–2020) strolling around his village in Paros, a small island far out in the Aegean Sea. Manolis was an impressive figure and so completely compelling that our visit has stayed with me, and for over a decade I've told the story of that day to anyone who would listen, again and again.

Manolis was the most respected (or reviled, depending on your politics) man in all of Greece, and well known throughout Europe primarily for a dazzling illegal action he and a friend undertook in 1941. While still a teenager, he climbed the Acropolis and tore down and destroyed the Nazi flag that had flown over Athens since German occupation forces marched into the city a month earlier, and then went on the run. This powerful symbolic act (an act of terrorism, according to the fascists) was magnified many times when the Nazis, determined to nip all opposition in the bud lest the virus of resistance spread, sentenced Manolis to death in absentia. Captured several months later, he was thrown into prison and tortured.

Manolis was ninety years old when we met up, a veteran of over seventy years of struggle for peace and justice. He'd been imprisoned by the German occupiers, the Italians, the Greek collaborators, and the Regime of the Colonels, adding up to more than a decade behind bars, as well as four years in exile. Manolis had been sentenced to death multiple times, charged with espionage, treason, and sabotage, and he had escaped prison more than once. He'd been the focus of widespread international protests and "Free Glezos!" campaigns over the years, which surely explained why Manolis was still alive and standing at the dock waving happily when I arrived.

We greeted each other warmly, exchanged presents, and walked arm in arm to a nearby cafe. Glezos had been an elected member of the Greek Parliament over several years representing different left-wing parties, and he'd been elected to the European Parliament as well, receiving more votes than anyone else in Greece. I asked him about his time in the Greek Parliament, and he said that each time he ran for office, and particularly when he was elected, it was always as part of a larger strategy and a bigger collective, a useful tactic for him and his comrades at specific times but never an end in itself. "I'm not a professional politician," he said. "I'm only interested in people collectively discovering their own power. That's the most important thing, and an entirely different undertaking from an individual or a party in power."[1]

His home was filled with mementos and awards, including a striking portrait of him painted and signed by Picasso. Manolis told me about several awards and recognitions he'd refused over the years because they were offered by "dictatorial" governments, he said, that only wanted to use him to legitimize their cruel regimes and burnish their own images.

When Manolis was elected president of the Community Council in Aperathu in 1986, he and his socialist/anarchist comrades created a radical experiment in far-reaching participatory democracy. They governed by consensus in a local assembly with forums reminiscent of the period of radical democracy in ancient Greece, only now everyone received a vote. They abolished all privileges for elected officials, developed a written constitution, and challenged the idea that "experts" or self-proclaimed leaders were better at running the town's affairs than the everyday ordinary people. They sought spontaneous cooperation, reciprocity, improvisation, experimentation, dialogue, popular education, and debate—all without hierarchy. These are the hallmarks of a robust *participatory* democracy, a term that became the watchword for the early years of the Student Nonviolent Coordinating Committee and Students for a Democratic Society in the US. Beyond the relatively anemic idea that democracy means voting now and then for someone who will exercise power more or less on your behalf and more or less in your name, this more immediate and direct democracy assumes that the people with the problems are also the people with the solutions, and that being engaged in the process of dealing face to face with our challenges will embolden and awaken a more enlightened polity. "Every cook can govern!" was a kind of theme and watchword. Everyone can be free.

We talked all that afternoon about the obstacles to revolution and freedom beyond the obvious power and evident ruthlessness of the capitalist class. For Manolis, a central problem was a serious and often unrecognized lack of confidence within ourselves. "Do you want to win?" he asked. Perhaps the prospect of real freedom frightens us, and we want nothing more than to accept easy answers and someone else's—the church, the state, the corporation, anyone else—judgment. "What would winning look like? And do we preempt disappointment by assuming we will lose anyway? We act sometimes like we're terrified of winning."

"We spend our lives in the presence of mayors and chiefs-of-police," he said, "of executives and bosses and managers, in the presence of all type and manner of hierarchy, and we adapt to finding ourselves lost in the pyramid—unseen, unheard, and summarily irrelevant." We become like the people in Dostoevsky's *The Grand Inquisitor*, dropping our powers of self-reliance and doubting that we could live without those authorities.[2] We worship authority in spite of ourselves, and soon enough we embrace our own passivity and apathy, becoming enslaved to a culture of obedience. "That's a core weakness," Manolis argued. We must break the straitjackets of conventional thinking—the fatal culture of obedience and conformity—grapple with the challenges of agency, live our freedom dreams here and now, take responsibility for the world, and refuse to hand power to the dictators, real or metaphoric.

Fear of freedom is the heart of Ray Bradbury's dystopic novel *Fahr-enheit 451*: Books have been outlawed and the fire department is charged with destroying them. The most remarkable explanation of why they participate in this nasty book-burning work comes from the fire chief, Captain Beatty—standing in for governors Ron DeSantis and Greg Abbott in our own time. Beatty points out that the people themselves demanded that the books be burned, because books with their "great welter of nouns and verbs and adjectives" make a simple world much too complicated to enjoy.[3] Complexity and contradiction, recognition of diversity, mutuality and compromise and dialogue, im-perfection, precariousness and ambiguity, all the basics of a full life as it's actually lived—these are the enemies of every form of fundamen-talism on earth. Totalitarians and autocrats, tyrants and bullies of every stripe and condition, have nothing to learn since all the answers are ready-made and at hand. They have nothing to lose since the goal is one-dimensional and rather simple: my way or no way, and a fight to the finish with the infidels. Freedom from adjectives and adverbs! Freedom from books!

Manolis Glezos was a lifelong freedom fighter, an anarchist, and a socialist. He embodied in his commitments and his actions the words of Mikhail Bakunin, the nineteenth-century socialist revolutionary and founder of collectivist anarchism: "Freedom without socialism is privilege and injustice; socialism without freedom is slavery and brutality."[4] Bakunin's motto, like Glezos's life, contains multitudes.

Anarchism has been persistently—and often intentionally—misun-derstood and misrepresented. Anarchy is chaos and frenzy and tumult, say the haters; anarchism is a synonym for nihilism; anarchists promote mobocracy. All of this is a worn-out collection of lazy clichés, none of it true, but the wildly popular cartoon image of the bearded loner with a look of scooped-out desperation in his eyes and a round black bomb sizzling under his heavy overcoat remains.

A more hopeful and a truer sense of anarchism can be found on display in a large and loving family, or a small, sparkling preschool, in mini-societies driven by norms of equality, mutual respect, interdependence, and reciprocity in which people share resources and care about and for one another. These spaces are not flawless, and the people in them are neither angels nor do they aspire to sainthood; they do embody, however, an intuitive sense of fairness worked out face to face, and they become sources of both freedom and mutual aid for one another. Individuals are understood to be works in progress—questioning, listening, falling down, fucking up, rising once more, learning, and continuously experimenting with and interrogating the world—with distinct capacities and interests and needs, and still members of a larger communal space. The prevailing ethic accounts for and corrects all chance/accidental disadvantages, from each according to ability, and to each according to need. There it is, imperfect to be sure: deeply human, a little off-kilter, and slightly dysfunctional by definition, a wild and in some sense universal model of everyday anarchy and commonsense socialism.

In a larger context, an authentically democratic society would invite people to discover or invent new ways to live, and new passages through which to make collective decisions—for example, Glezos's forums and assemblies in Aperathu; mutual aid networks organized spontaneously by citizens after Hurricane Maria; Truth and Reconciliation Commissions in South Africa; or Citizenship Schools in the segregated South. With genuine power in their hands, people learn—quite rapidly—to make smart and socially useful decisions, and also to assume real responsibility for carrying out their collectively developed resolutions. The challenge is to show people who've been traditionally ignored or excluded that their involvement will have meaning and be effective, and that their ideas will be respected; the greater hazard is not too much but too little participation.

None of this is easy, of course, and it's made much more difficult in a culture infused with savage competition and toxic individualism. I'm reminded of William Golding's *Lord of the Flies*, required reading for millions of American teenagers for decades—and no wonder. The book promotes a philosophy that assumes the "darkness of man's heart," the fundamental evil simmering just beneath our skin, and the necessity of a powerful state to curb and control our savage, anarchist instincts.[5] Surely you know the basic outline: several English schoolboys survive a plane crash and find themselves on a desert island; they initially form a kind of democracy with agreed-upon rules, but, left to themselves and without the civilizing authority of modern society, they quickly and easily descend into barbarous anarchy. When things have spun completely out of control—murder and mayhem—a British naval officer arrives in his crisp uniform, along with a promise that order will be restored and things will be set right.

I read the book in high school and disliked it immediately; it felt to me like anti-kid propaganda. Of course, I didn't know the half of it, and I didn't look at it again for years. Still, it was inescapable, partly because everyone else had read it, and partly because it was such a steady reference and mainstay in our culture: people are basically bad, left to ourselves we're all beasts, and thank God for law and order.

I picked it up again years later because I met a novelist at the University of Hawai'i who challenged its assumptions so thoroughly that I wanted to take another peek. Kenzaburo Oe and I were in the same visiting-scholar cohort, and we chatted at our occasional lunches together. I'd not read his novels at that point; this was before he won the 1994 Nobel Prize for Literature and before his books were widely available in English. I discovered a book he wrote as a student in 1958 called *Nip the Buds, Shoot the Kids*, and I devoured it—a perfect antidote to Golding's dark imagination. Here is the story of a small band of kids labeled "juvenile delinquents" evacuated from Tokyo during World War II to a remote mountain village where they're hated by the superstitious and cruel inhabitants. When the fear of plague erupts, the villagers flee in the night, and the children are abandoned and barricaded inside the village to die. But in that autonomous and free space the juvenile delinquents discover their deep humanity as they build a purposeful community of self-respect, mutual aid, repair, and love. For Kenzaburo Oe, the kids were doing the best they could while civilization was unleashing atomic bombs and other weapons of mass destruction on one another, and "maddened adults ran riot in the streets."[6] Oe goes through the looking glass and turns *Lord of the Flies* on its head. I was so grateful.

<hr/>

Manolis was witness and testifier to the twentieth century, arguably the bloodiest in human history by far. Not to be outdone, the twenty-first is on a steady path of continuing the ruin, and perhaps surpassing it. The "Traders' War" (World War I), the Holocaust in Europe, colonial arrogance and occupation, genocides, imperialism's deadly delusions, carpet bombing, and nuclear weapons brandished everywhere and actually unleashed, *twice*, by the US on Japanese cities—all of this madness marched under the banner of "freedom."

Popular aspirations for freedom in the twentieth century also fueled revolutionary fervor and rebellion, but it's fair to say that those hopes and desires were largely betrayed and those passions perverted by a wide range of forces: violent counterrevolutions and immediate and relentless attacks by capitalist armies, as well as sabotage and disruption from within, cooptation by capital, oppressive autocratic rule, corruption, deceit, technological shifts, neoliberal and neo-imperialist meddling, and murder and mayhem. We are far, far away from the ideal of freedom so many generations fought and sacrificed to achieve; there's a lot of work to do. A lot. And that work—organizing, studying, staying awake and alert, taking action, building the social justice movements—is in part a debt we owe to all those who struggled toward freedom before us, all those who tried to make history in the world as it was, and in circumstances that were decidedly not of their choosing. They made mistakes, of course, and we make them too; I think they're sorry, and I'm sorry too. There are so many, many things that can't be undone— but I'm glad we fought, and I wish we'd won.

The reality of our predicament, from the primitive accumulation of capital to the current crisis of imperialism, has a name: colonialism, the super-exploitation of the Global South, the Third World outside and inside the borders of advanced capitalism. And the super-profits reaped by colonialist policies provided the material basis for opportunism: anesthetizing privilege and what Marx called the aristocracy of labor inside the advanced capitalist countries. Some First World Marxists, claiming a deeper insight than the reality before their eyes, continue to belittle the anticolonial, anti-racist struggle as subordinate to the general working-class struggle within the US—a tragic, repeating, and avoidable mistake.

Our freedom dreams are still alive, and the shortcomings of past struggles can provide teachable moments and even inspiration for us if we face them with open hearts and open eyes, not as self-righteous judges of our forebears and our ancestors, but as comrades and students. We can work hard to expand our visionary horizons, to break with the stale models from the past or the anemic alternatives that are on easy offer today, and then dive into the wreckage and swim as hard as we can toward a distant and indistinct horizon. "Western democracy"—that is, rule by casino capitalism and military-bloated states—has no answers to our freedom dreams. And we must remember that states are never willingly involved with expanding the arena of human freedom; in fact, states have grown steadily more powerful, more intrusive, more repressive, and more capable and willing to control people as they facilitate the accelerating extraction of labor, resources, and more and more profits for the few—and the beat goes on.

The past is past. The new and the unknown beckon as we rise up to follow a useful and well-worn cadence: try, fail, try again, fail again, fail better. That catchy rhythm appears five separate times in Samuel Beckett's 1983 novella *Worstward Ho*, and the first time it goes like this: "Ever tried. Ever failed. No matter. Try again. Fail again. Fail better."[7] I love that, and I chant it quietly as I make my wobbly way through the day.

Our recently departed comrade William Rivers Pitt noted that we are

once again at a crossroads at midnight with a blood moon rising. Down one road lies fire, flood, famine, failure and the final triumph of greed. What awaits down the other road is unknown, a mystery to be solved one gentle step at a time. The road we have been on is littered with bones and sorrow. The road we must take is strange, and new, and dangerous, and difficult. There are no promises, other than it will be—by dint of our collective will—better than the way that is failing before our eyes. This crossroads is freedom distilled, and the time to choose is now.[8]

If you're not convinced that we'd be better off as a society or as a people if everyone participated equally in governing, you're not alone. Undoubtedly many of us would quickly fall back on conventional wisdom or on the insistent dogma of common sense or on mindless group-think, which means that our decisions would not move us closer to justice or balance or harmony or peace or fairness or freedom. Your skepticism is sensible.

Any radical or revolutionary change is a process of reimagining and rebuilding, challenging the dominant common sense and making surprising new connections. I once had a conversation about prison abolition with a friend who had been in state prison for over a decade. We were meeting in the prison visiting area, and she was generally sympathetic to the concept as an idea or a theory but doubted its practicality. "Listen," she said at one point, half-joking, "you don't want some of these folks on the street." We laughed, but then took our conversation a step further, imagining what kind of society we would have to build, asking what kind of culture we would need to nourish and sustain, and what kind of people we would need to become in order for us to want "some of these folks on the street," and prison abolition more than a dream? Prison abolition is a complex and profound transformational ideal—it's not a simple matter of unlocking a gate into the world as it is. It's a matter of ordinary people becoming extraordinary, changing ourselves in order to change the world. People telling their truths, discovering their own agency and their own collective power is, as Manolis Glezos argues, both earth shaking and world building. Poet Muriel Rukeyser famously asked, "What would happen if one woman told the truth about her life?" Her answer: "The world would split open."[9]

Yes, we need more involvement, fuller participation, more whole-hearted engagement, and, yes, ordinary people like you and me are quite capable of building a robust democracy in spite of what the ruling barbarians claim. But not with the status quo intact and unchanged, not with individualism and hypercompetition and racism and sexism encoded and enforced, not with militarism at the center of foreign relations and materialism and consumerism the national religion. In struggling toward participatory democracy, we need to transform ourselves, becoming new people worthy of the new society we're midwifing and helping to bring into the world. We will need to build—brick by brick—an anti-oppressive culture, an anti-exploitative economy, an education for free people that lifts up the arts of liberty.

There will surely be lots of disagreement and some dysfunction, but, compared to the current chaos and deadly status quo, what a relief!

Today talk of freedom is pervasive: free trade and the free world, free markets and free exchange, freedom to refuse stay-at-home orders, especially if you're white, and parade unmasked and armed at state capitols. But it often feels abstract and distant, weirdly off-kilter, and assumed but never really available for active or concrete participation. Personal freedom—our self-proclaimed and celebrated rights and choices, our assumed autonomy and insistent independence—is a paradox: free to drive anywhere, we find ourselves stuck in traffic; free to speak our minds, we don't have much to say; free to choose, we feel oddly entangled; free to vote for any candidate, we experience a Tweedledum/Tweedledummer befuddlement.

The "freedom to choose" is rendered in particularly savage terms in Haruku Murakami's novel *Colorless Tsukuru Tazaki*. A character named

Aka, who founded a human resource training company, describes his job as teaching employees how to fit in, and offers an example to his old friend Tsukura:

> It's the first thing I always say at our new employee training seminars. I gaze around the room, pick one person, and have him stand up. And this is what I say: I have some good news for you, and some bad news. The bad news first. We're going to have to rip off either your fingernails or your toenails with pliers. I'm sorry, but it's already decided. It can't be changed. I pull out a huge, scary pair of pliers from my briefcase and show them to everybody. Slowly, making sure everybody gets a good look. And then I say: Here's the good news. You have the freedom to choose which it's going to be—your fingernails, or your toenails. So, which will it be? You have ten seconds to make up your mind. If you're unable to decide, we'll rip off both your fingernails and your toenails. I start the count. At about eight seconds most people say, "The toes." Okay, I say, toenails it is . . . But . . . Why did you choose your toes and not your fingers? The person usually says, "I don't know. I think they probably hurt the same. But since I had to choose one, I went with the toes." I turn to him and warmly applaud him. And I say, Welcome to the real world. . . . " He continues, "Each of us is given the freedom to choose. . . . That's the point of the story."[10]

Most of us, of course, are entirely dependent on others for a living; we have no voice and no vote in what will be produced, why or how, or who makes the rules and who profits. Without that power, our freedom is an anemic fantasy. The myth that "anyone can succeed under capitalism" is a club in the hands of power: "Your poverty, your shitty job, your homelessness are your problem and your own failures—why didn't you work harder?" The myth stretches itself and extends: since one person can accomplish something, everyone could have accomplished that same thing. This is illogical and ridiculous. One person can become chairman of United Airlines, but everyone can't; if one person gets a discount because she knows the cashier, everyone getting a discount would put the place out of business; one person can take a book from the library and fail to return it, but if everyone does that, there's no library.

We experience the flattening impacts of white supremacy, of sexism, of violence and structural forms of injustice that are so deeply a part of our national heritage and character, and, as well, the pacifying effects of a mass consumer society, the sense of being manipulated, lied to, shaped, and used by powerful forces. We hear all around us market fundamentalists defending their "freedom" to extract profits through capitalist markets unfettered by public input or government regulation, all the while promoting the idea that the purest forms of freedom and democratic living can be easily reduced to a question of shopping. We're said to be free, but when the hurricanes and wildfires and rising seas threaten to engulf us, we feel like bugs in a glass bowl: vulnerable, endangered, powerless, and clamoring helplessly up and down the walls.

We're not entirely determined, of course, but neither do we enjoy absolute liberty and unrestricted choice. No one chooses their parents, to take an obvious example; no one chooses a nation or a tribe to be born into. We are, in Hannah Arendt's phrase, "free and fated; fated and free."[11] Like everyone else we're thrust into a going world, a world already underway and not at all of our own making, and somehow we must choose who and how to be in this brief crack of light—closing our eyes tight, refusing to see any options whatsoever, is itself a kind of choosing. In some situations, we might accede, in others, refuse. So, here we are: we are situated; and we are free. And we are dizzy.

Increasingly scientists who examine the timeline of the Earth, from the Paleozoic to the Jurassic to the Holocene and all points before and since, refer to the present time as the Anthropocene, the age of humans. This is the era characterized by dramatic human-induced, planetary-scale changes, the era of nuclear power and massive carbon extraction. A century ago—and, for many, even a decade ago or right now—common sense said that nature was too big to react to any human influence. The ocean was infinite, the atmosphere boundless. Anyone who believes that today is delusional, or more likely blinded by the ideology of the "free market." The collision with a giant asteroid did away with the dinosaurs, but human impact may prove to be a much greater threat to human life on Earth, and an insanely myopic sense of "freedom" is invoked to fuel the Death Star.

Let's imagine advancing beyond the predatory phase in human affairs, envisioning a place of more, not less, participatory democracy, more, not less, economic justice, more respect for civil liberties and more tolerance for private lives, more popular education and deep study, more public culture and a much-expanded commons, more joyous shared space, more peace and dialogue and disarmament and camaraderie and fellowship and sisterhood and solidarity and mutual reconciliation and aid. More freedom for all, not just a few. Let's imagine a world without prisons and think about what kind of society we would need to build to make that dream a reality. Now imagine a world without war, a world without soldiers and police. A world without advertising! Let's participate now in efforts to create and support worker-owned enterprises, cooperatives, collectives, and unions through negotiation where possible and occupations, seizures, and takeovers where necessary. And let's mobilize messy, raucous, and lengthy community meetings where everyone learns to make a meal (vegetable stir-fry, tortillas, lentil soup, pasta salad) from scratch, avoids looking at a clock or a screen, and considers how much stuff is too much stuff.

Imagine the burden and the satisfaction of engaging in whatever we collectively deem to be the common good. Imagine focusing our attention and weighing in about issues that often seem distant or obscure or somehow best handled by the experts: food production and distribution, child- and eldercare, transportation, education, housing, justice, community health, infrastructure development, neighborhood gardens and parks and murals. Imagine what it would mean to have voluntary and universal community service, say, at eighteen, everyone choosing to devote a year of service in one of ten areas determined of, by, and for the people—we'd likely have more powerful investments and opinions and political priorities about who we are and what we want to become. And then imagine keeping it growing year after year: a year of voluntary service at twenty-eight, thirty-eight, forty-eight, and fifty-eight. We'd all be better for it, and it might help us to collectively create a vibrant, robust, and authentically participatory democracy.

This brings to mind another paradox of freedom, which connects back to Reflection Two: when the oppressed free themselves, their activity frees the oppressors as well. The abolition of slavery freed the enslaved workers from bondage, true, and it simultaneously freed slave-owners from their evil business, and from the anxiety of wondering when payback would come; when Black people are free, white people can leave behind their shaky pretense of superiority with all its attendant loneliness and stress; when women get free, men will be freed from clinging desperately to their precarious and alienating privileges. Freedom is large, generous, and generative—and it's free for all.

5

TRUTH AND RECONCILIATION
AND FREEDOM

"COMO TÚ"

Yo, como tú,
amo el amor, la vida, el dulce encanto
de las cosas, el paisaje
celeste de los días de enero.
También mi sangre bulle
y río por los ojos
que han conocido el brote de las lágrimas.
Creo que el mundo es bello,
que la poesía es como el pan, de todos.
Y que mis venas no terminan en mí
sino en la sangre unánime
de los que luchan por la vida,
el amor,
las cosas,
el paisaje y el pan,
la poesía de todos.

—ROQUE DALTON

"LIKE YOU"

Like you I
love love, life, the sweet smell
of things, the sky-blue
landscape of January days.
And my blood boils up
and I laugh through eyes
that have known the buds of tears.
I believe the world is beautiful
and that poetry, like bread, is for everyone.
And that my veins don't end in me
but in the unanimous blood

of those who struggle for life,
love,
little things,
landscape and bread,
the poetry of everyone.

—ROQUE DALTON

> If we don't try to tell the truth—complex, dynamic, and layered—
> we're trapped in a bughouse, and bedlam surrounds us; if we don't
> search for the truth, we can't realistically overcome obstacles, or ef-
> fectively resist harm; if we don't wrestle with the truth, we're floating
> on a sea of lies, either wobbling through a relativistic fantasy land or
> staring unblinkingly at a single blinding lightbulb. Either way, we're
> trapped—we aren't learning, and we aren't free. Take a moment and
> describe a time when you tried to tell the truth as you understood
> it—raw and unvarnished, perhaps risky and a bit subversive—and you
> were met with hostility. What did you say or do then?

— REFLECTION FIVE: FREEDOM, TRUTH, AND REPAIR —

In Bertolt Brecht's 1938 play *Galileo*, the astronomer's breathtaking
discoveries about the movement of the planets and the stars fire a
desire to change the world: "The cities are narrow and so are the
brains," he declares boldly. "Superstition and plague. But now the
word is: since it is so, it does not remain so. For everything moves, my
friend."[1] Galileo wants to free himself and others from the prison of
ignorance and delusion that constrains them all, and his truth-telling
is revolutionary, challenging the establishment in the realm of its
own authority—the church, after all, constructs the human journey
as a sanctioned and planned voyage, the steps entirely mapped out in
advance with clockwork precision and mathematical certainty. All
the support anyone needs abides in the institution of the church itself.
Kings are meant to rule, and peasants to obey. Because free inquiry
is not authorized, and free thought or free choice are not sanctioned,
benighted human beings are imprisoned in foolishness and stupidity.

Galileo resolves to set us free, tilting against the unfreedom of lies and myths and credulousness.

In 1610, the nonfictional, flesh-and-blood Galileo published "Starry Messenger," describing his observations made with a modern and more powerful telescope, and continued to provide further evidence supporting Copernicus's heliocentric theory. He was asked to stop but he wouldn't, and when the church had had enough, he was dragged before the Roman Inquisition in 1633, convicted of being "vehemently suspect of heresy," and sentenced to house arrest until his lonely death in 1642.[2]

Clearly more than theories of astronomy were at stake. The ideas, surely, but also the joy, the excitement, and the reckless hope all mark Galileo as a free thinker and a freedom fighter—after all, he could have written a book, as Copernicus did, and left it at that. But he kept pushing, not only for his ideas and his right to interrogate the world but also for everyone to experience the liberation—the freedom—that is impossible without knowledge and awareness. No one can be free with their head buried in the sand.

In Brecht's play, Galileo's struggle was punctuated with hope and despair, pain and pressure, and when he finally capitulated to the exquisite torture of the Inquisition, denouncing *what he knew to be true*, he was received back "into the ranks of the faithful" by the church, even as he was exiled from humanity—by his own words. In the end, he was confronted by a former student, one of his crest-fallen disciples: "Many on all sides followed you with their eyes and ears," the student said, "believing that you stood, not only for a particular view of the movement of the stars, but even more for the liberty of teaching—in all fields. Not then for any particular thoughts, but for the right to think at all. Which is in dispute."[3] The right to imagine and discuss complex and dynamic truths, the right to think at all, freedom and the liberty of teaching—something that's in deep dispute in our schools and classrooms now, and in the streets as well.

These subversive ideas walk hand in hand with Fyodor Dostoevsky's "The Grand Inquisitor," a well-known story-within-the-story from *The Brothers Karamazov*, written by the fictional character Ivan Fyodorovich. According to Ivan's parable, Jesus has returned to Earth at the time of the Spanish Inquisition, and when he is arrested and sentenced to be executed, the Grand Inquisitor visits him in his cell to explain that his return interferes with the wide and growing influence of the Church. Jesus had his chance when he met Satan in the desert and rejected the three temptations—to turn stones into bread, to fall from the temple and be saved by angels, and to rule over the world—in favor of human freedom. Jesus's inaction doomed people to suffer; freedom was too great a burden for most. The Church offered people what they really wanted: doctrine, dogma, blind faith, easy answers, and certainty. And the Inquisition was the instrument to enforce that faith: "And men rejoice at being led like cattle again, with the terrible gift of freedom that brought them so much suffering removed from them."[4]

The terrible gift of freedom brings to my mind a notable story about the French philosopher Jean-Paul Sartre during World War II and the German occupation. In my retelling, a student had come to him with a formidable dilemma. "My mother is deathly ill," the student explained, "and I'm responsible for her care, but my father is collaborating with the Nazis, and in order to account for that crime, I feel I must join the Resistance—what should I do?" After much consideration and discussion of pros and cons, Sartre told the student, *You must choose.* "I know, of course, I know I must choose, and you're the great philosopher which is why I came to you. Please offer me some wisdom to help me choose." *Well,* Sartre continued, *that is precisely the difficulty of every authentic choice—in fact, the problem of freedom itself. Every yes is a no, every no, a yes, and you yourself—no one else—are responsible for the choices you make. You must choose.* "You've been no help to me at all!" cried the indignant student. "I will go instead to a priest!" *Very well,* Sartre responded. *Which priest will you choose?*

I think of this story whenever I'm asked for a specific kind of advice—for example, when my twenty-year-old niece asked me if I thought she should move in with her boyfriend. Now there's a loaded question for an uncle. *Why am I your priest, and not your mother* (my sister), *or your grandmother* (my mother)? I asked. *So,* she responded, *you think it's OK, right?* I didn't say that, but clearly she chose me as her priest because she assumed, given all she knows about my life and my values, that her weird uncle would be all for it, whereas her mom or her grandmother? Maybe not so much. The young adults wanted to move in together, and she chose the priest who, she assumed, aligned with what she already knew she wanted. She didn't want advice; she wanted the terrible gift of freedom removed. Sartre is saying that we pick our priests, we choose our gods and our masters, hoping and believing that they will take the *terrible gift of freedom* off our hands. By dispersing the responsibility, we hope to blame the consequences of our actions on others.

Freedom is a precious good and also a burden of responsibility. These characters and images reveal powerful forces that challenge and restrict human freedom. Truth is messy and complicated and often elusive, but where the pursuit of complex and fugitive truths is recognized and acted upon, we gain some measure of control over ourselves, and perhaps our futures; where truth is obstructed, freedom shrivels and dies. On the one hand, brute force, intimidation, and torture can destroy freedom; on the other hand, mystification, deception, and illusion can do that nasty work as well. Both are impediments, and yet in many ways the more problematic obstacle is the imposition of dogma and orthodoxy—the invisible shackles wrapped around our minds, which can be harder to see, and then more difficult to resist.

Truth and reconciliation are sequential—you simply cannot successfully harmonize with a lie forever.

It's no wonder, then, that America's original sin—the deep, unhealed wound of racism and white supremacy—haunts the land to this day, rising up in new and terrible forms generation after generation. The US refuses to tell the truth, to see the truth, to hear the truth, and to finally grapple with the truth. America refuses to face history and itself. And without experiencing the truth of the past, there can be no authentic resolution for today, and no hope for a just or peaceable future.

The honest origin story begins by rejecting all the hazardous myths manufactured by the powerful to justify their position on this land: America is the land of the free and the home of the brave they claim— but it's untrue; America is a nation of laws—but the foundational lawlessness of the law itself is its most striking feature. America was created by hard-working free-thinkers—also false; America is a "nation of immigrants," a myth that erases and falsifies the rotten foundations of settler colonialism that we all stand on, precariously. Of course, there were (and are) brave and brilliant individuals in every country and era; there were and are large communities of immigrants. But holding this as frame and fortune obliterates the most obvious but profoundly inconvenient truths: this country is built on invasion and occupation, slave-driving and slave-breeding, land-stealing and genocide.

Land theft, slavery and the slave trade, in reality, provided the initial wealth necessary to launch the capitalist project. Karl Marx called this the "primitive accumulation" of capital, needed to give a boost to early factories, shipping, and trade.[5] So the very foundation of western wealth is built firmly on the backs of stolen Black bodies, stolen Native land, and the wholesale murder of Indigenous human beings.

The US is a settler-colonial colossus whose founders were invaders and conquerors, mercenaries and human traffickers, kidnappers and thieves, a mob of murderers who committed one of the most massive genocides in the history of the world—violence in the service of wealth accumulation is the national calling card. In their mad rush for profits (gold fever, land fever), the destroyers wiped out entire peoples and razed the vast forests of North America in a colossal environmental crime; they spoiled rivers and streams and decimated magnificent species like the redwoods and the North American buffalo. The wealth and the power of the US derives from armed robbery, serial murder, stolen land, and forced labor—that's not hyperbole. That's legacy. And we cannot be free without facing that hard truth.

In his monumental *Black Reconstruction in America*, W. E. B. Du Bois notes, "Nations reel and stagger on their way; they make hideous mistakes; they commit frightful wrongs; they do great and beautiful things." He then asks a question we ought to repeat again and again: "And shall we not best guide humanity by telling the truth about all this, so far as the truth is ascertainable?"[6] James Baldwin takes another step into understanding truth and memory and self-knowledge: "Whoever cannot tell himself the truth about his past is trapped in it, is immobilized in the prison of his undiscovered self. . . . We know how a person, in such a paralysis, is unable to assess either his weaknesses or his strengths, and how frequently indeed he mistakes one for the other." Baldwin then takes the personal back to the social: "This is also true of nations." We are trapped, imprisoned, and unfree without a sustained search for the truth.[7]

Facing the facts—the crimes and the horror—is not, as the powerful say over and over, an exercise to promote guilt or self-loathing. Just the opposite: there's no reason to feel guilty about cruelties you didn't commit, only a responsibility to repair the legacy of those crimes. Facing history and facing ourselves opens a path to a more generous and capacious sense of humanity as well as an enlarged field of action. We can't do a thing about the fact of slavery; we can, however, do a thousand things to abolish the afterlife of slavery—right here, right now. And that afterlife is not just the burden of the descendants of the enslaved workers; it's primarily the burden of those who received the unjustly accumulated wealth. Those riches were and are passed down through special deals like the "land rush" that opened Native territories and encouraged white homesteads, or the GI Bill offering housing for white veterans only. It includes greater freedom of movement for white people as well as schools with better facilities and curricula that glorify an imagined white history. To ask Black people to forget about the past and start from now would only be just if we also asked white people to forgo all these accumulated privileges from the past, the factors that allowed so many to be born on third base and imagine themselves to be fabulous as they waltzed home.

And the payoff for abolishing the afterlife of slavery is the possibility of a more peaceful, free, just, and joyful life for all of us. Liberal opportunists disrespect people (white and Black) when they assume that the only motivation for good behavior is narrow, short-term self-interest.

We're not stupid: our real interest lies in a just and balanced society. If we don't do the things we could do now—opening our eyes, facing facts forthrightly, acting on what the known demands of us—we ensure that the ghosts of the past will remain animated and dangerous.

The ghosts are all here, dancing in our heads, taunting us, and killing us. Jose Saramago, the Portuguese Nobel laureate who published his dazzling novel *Blindness* in 1995, said at the time, "Western societies became increasingly blind, because instead of tackling the big problems, we preferred to see less."[8] And it's true: climate change, forced migrations, starvation, infant mortality, child poverty, endless war—we prefer to see less. We are suffering, then, a pandemic of blindness.

The gun-wielding white men parading at statehouses in Michigan and Arizona are self-described freedom lovers: this is the exceptional nation, they repeat, and we are the reddest of red-blooded American patriots. They are tragically blinded by the myth of patriotism. Willful blindness, that deep, deep American sleep of denial, cannot make us free. It can only entangle us further, casting us into a darker dungeon.

In 1942, students at the University of Munich formed the "White Rose," an underground resistance to Adolph Hitler and the Third Reich; when they were uncovered and captured, they claimed to be German patriots even as they were denounced by the regime as "degenerate rogues" and sentenced to prison or death. At the Nuremberg trials after World War II, several Nazis pointed out (accurately, but to no avail) that they obeyed not only orders but also the law and were therefore simply doing their patriotic duty as Germans.

In 1962, a group of anti-communist Cubans, all self-styled patriots backed by the US CIA, launched an invasion of the island-nation from Florida in an attempt to overthrow the revolutionary government. They were defeated at the Bay of Pigs by another group of Cubans, mobilized under the banner "Patria o Muerte," who thought of themselves, naturally, as patriots.

A self-described patriot in Shanghai told me years ago that "the student riots in 1989 were the work of foreign agents and local traitors." More recently, I met a Chinese graduate student at Harvard who said that the students who led the Tiananmen Square uprising were the "true Chinese patriots." And I had a lengthy back-and-forth at the University of Southern Georgia some years ago with a man wearing a jacket emblazoned with a Confederate Battle Flag and a "Tea Party Patriot" patch. I pointed out that the Confederacy was organized by traitors—not patriots—willing to blow up the nation in defense of the "right" to own other human beings. He disagreed.

Wherever you start and however you look, patriotism is inevitably elusive and always entangled in context: historical flow, cultural surround, political perspective. It's a wobbly concept at best, debatable and necessarily occupying a contested space—the young students of Parkland, Florida, stare over a barricade at the irascible NRA leadership, each claiming the shiny mantle of patriotism; National Football League team owners lock out Colin Kaepernick in the name of patriotism and decree that players must stand respectfully during the playing of the National Anthem, an enforced display of patriotism that is a long-standing hallmark of authoritarianism and autocracy.

The instinct and desire to belong to something larger than oneself—a people, say, or a singular nation—is common; the longing for membership in a distinctive group with clear boundaries and stable expectations is clear. But it isn't freedom. I don't underestimate the sense of pleasure and solace that accompanies an embrace of patriotism, and I find the enthusiasm for a group identity, while troubling, understandable. But the pitfalls of patriotism are everywhere, and at some point, those hazards must be faced.

To begin, patriotism is not, and can never aspire to be, a universal moral code like "Love thy neighbor as thyself," or "Do unto others as you would have others do unto you." Patriotism is always embedded in the local and can never express a general principle or a common human aspiration. After all, if tomorrow everyone on earth claimed to be a fierce and focused patriot of their current country of residence,

20 percent of the world's people would be Chinese patriots, and 4.4 percent would be patriotic Americans.

Patriotism is tied to the questionable proposition of the modern state—something that is only a few hundred years old in the many thousands of years of human history. The construction of the state, the imagined loyalty to a geographical region, was part of the capitalist project. And in making that move, ruling classes fought hard to obliterate local customs and languages. Even today, countries like Spain and France and China and the US contain within them numerous languages and practices that resist the homogenizing demands of the state.

When then mayor Rudy Giuliani was asked if waterboarding human beings constitutes torture, he gave the classic patriotic/nationalist response: "It depends on who does it."[9] In his own mind, he was surely acting as a textbook patriot, supporting the country and offering a rigorous defense against enemies or detractors. But note that, to the patriot, actions are held to be good in some hands and bad in others, depending solely on who commits the outrage. Torture, assassinations, bombing civilians, forced confessions, invasion and occupation, constant state surveillance, involuntary servitude, hostage-taking, vengeance, imprisonment without trial—all of this and more is judged according to the patriotic nationalist by a single criterion: who did it. Patriotism, then, dulls the imagination, obscures reality, entraps and imprisons all of us in a fantasy, anesthetizes some people, and causes moral blindness or ethical amnesia in others.

Our country was founded on slavery and genocide—as noted, it's at the center of our American character and country. Many self-defined patriots want to deny or forget that agonizing, painful, and horrifying part of our collective story, but the cost of not remembering can be excruciating as well; calculated unconsciousness, sham innocence, and stubborn silence in the name of patriotism and freedom assure that the racial wounds will never heal, the horror will abide. The tragedy, shame, and pain of this country—including kidnapping, slavery, rape, murder, genocide, torture, terrorism, predation, exploitation and oppression, degradation and humiliation—are foundational, linked, and evolving. Slavery begets lynching begets Jim Crow and segregation and voter suppression and redlining and on and on to mass incarceration. Living on myths and lies guarantees an unhappy life of fear and precarity, awaiting the social correction and the impending payback that's sure to come. Telling the truth will free up all that vast and squandered energy that's now spent shoring up the eroding myths and policing the boundaries of reality.

James Baldwin pointed out that the "American Negro has the great advantage of having never believed the collection of myths to which white Americans cling: that their ancestors were all freedom-loving heroes, that they were born in the greatest country the world has ever seen, or that Americans are invincible in battle and wise in peace, that Americans have always dealt honorably with Mexicans and Indians. . . . [Our] tendency has really been . . . to dismiss white people as the slightly mad victims of their own brainwashing."[10] White identity politics has always simply called itself "American."

"If we have to use force," former US secretary of state Madeleine Albright famously said, "it is because we are America. We are the indispensable nation."[11] Not only exceptional but now somehow indispensable as well. A benign interpretation of that extravagant claim might visualize the country as a shining city on the hill, the very paragon of democracy and freedom; a more realistic assessment might see the US astride the world like Colossus, holding itself exempt from international agreements like the International Criminal Court and the Paris Climate Accords, above the laws that govern others, particularly concerning the use of lethal force. Because we are the unambiguous model of virtue and righteousness, our actions are always good; because our actions are always good, we are not subject to the ordinary rules that apply to all others—"we are the indispensable nation." So, while Russian meddling in US elections is widely seen as outrageous (and it is), US meddling in elections from Honduras and Venezuela to Ukraine and Cyprus is (if US patriots even bother to notice) not so bad. The hypocrisy and naked narcissism are breathtaking.

Patriotism—the modern-day Grand Inquisitor—promises a steady anchor and a convenient road map, but it is, in reality, entirely unstable.

Anyone wrapped in the flag or donning the crown of patriotism would be well advised to pause before being lulled into a sense of settled comfort, or any fuzzy familiar feeling of self-righteousness. The wheel turns and people stumble into the vortex of a dynamic, living history, the crown suddenly tarnished or askew, the banner singed and torn, and are then required to make their wobbly ways without the false security patriotism promises.

All of this might move us to note that every human being is indigenous to planet Earth, and that there is, therefore, no such thing as a foreigner. We might work, then, to replace national patriotism with human solidarity—*sin fronteras*—in the spirit of Chicago's poet laureate Gwendolyn Brooks: "We are each other's harvest: / we are each other's / business: / we are each other's / magnitude and bond."[12]

After the January 6 uprising in the US Capitol, the president declared that we had almost lost "our democracy." He imagined some mythical, glorified democracy, perhaps the democracy practiced in ancient Athens for most of its history, which was, on close examination, limited to a small sector of propertied men—not so different from the US today. A more truthful evaluation would widen the lens and look at the US, not simply as the geographic area governed within established and designated borders but an entire world system that includes most of Latin America and large parts of Asia and Africa and Europe. Looked at in this way, "our democracy" was lost at the start, and it remains wounded, contingent, and tentative at best. If the people of Chile elect a socialist president, as they did in 1970, the US national security advisor, Henry Kissinger, rejects the popular vote, declaring, "I don't see why we have to stand by and watch a country go Communist because of the irresponsibility of its own people."[13] And so it goes throughout the world—countries that toe the line of US domination are declared "democracies," while those that decide otherwise are undermined, subverted, and attacked.

The crowd that stormed the Capitol in January 2021 was a fascist mob, to be sure. And fascism can be understood as a situation in which the banal, everyday practices of colonial administration—direct and violent control—come home to roost in the imperial center. Mussolini's fascism was Italian military practices in Libya domesticated to the home country; Spain's was a copy of the Spanish-Moroccan regime; Hitler's desecration of Europe mimicked the practices of Europe in Africa to, as Sven Lindqvist puts it, "exterminate all the brutes."[14] We should question whether the reproduction of our privileged island as the imperial center in order to recover "our democracy" is good enough (or good at all), and how we might encourage and struggle toward real democracy, participatory radical democracy and freedom itself, for ourselves and for everyone everywhere.

After every heartbreaking and horrible school shooting, we hear the conservative argument that "guns don't kill people, people kill people," and that any restrictions on weapons is an attack on freedom. The liberal argument answers that ordinary people should not have access to assault rifles or "military grade" weapons like the AR-15 and others built with a fully automatic capacity. But the grisly, unconsidered assumption of the liberals is that while these weapons of mass death should not be used to spray innocent students at a school in Connecticut or Florida or Texas, they are understood to be appropriate for spraying innocent people in Iraq, Afghanistan, Palestine, or Libya. Dressing young people up in military uniforms and attempting to rebrand mass murder as "service" is, upon the slightest reflection, villainous.

Too often, our good intentions, our humanitarian impulses, stop at the US border, or with merely the symptoms, and fail to dig deeper into why these things are happening and what causes need to be rooted out for an actual resolution. Truth, repair, reconciliation.

We swim in a culture of untruth, bathed day in and day out in a river of lies. The MAGA nonsense, the claims of stolen elections, the fake news, and alternative facts are only the tip of a gigantic iceberg of frozen lies. Long before "truthiness" there was advertising, which calls itself an "industry" and is nothing more than a many-billion-dollar sham/scam—prevarication at an industrial scale. We've become accustomed to having upward of four hundred lies a day, dressed in bright colors and happy talk, wash over us in a steady stream; we can even find ourselves with our eyes blank and our mouths open, admiring some of the cleverer mini-narratives or taglines. "Just do it!"

And, of course, it's a truism: governments lie. Some governments lie all the time, and all governments lie some of the time. When our government has been caught in its most egregious lies recently, it responds with neither apology nor contrition, and instead goes on the attack—just ask Julian Assange, Jeffrey Sterling, Edward Snowden, Reality Winner, Chelsea Manning, John Kiriakou, Shamai Leibowitz, Stephen Jin-Woo Kim, James Hitselberger, or any of the other brave people who blew the whistle and paid the price.

Even scientific facts, in a dramatically different register, are unstable and in need of continual revision. Our common sense is upended again and again, and what we took to be solid one day melts into air the next. The desire for certainty in an uncertain world is understandable; the impulse to categorize, sort, label, and fix is powerful—but it's not science. And it's not truth.

The scientific enterprise is in reality built on challenging, disproving, rethinking, and revising. Evidence, evidence, and then more evidence is marshaled to show the inadequacy of what we once held to be true. Additional evidence, new arguments and explanations replace the old. You may find this discouraging, if your temperament is gloomy, or you may see within it the essence of freedom—the dynamic, unsettling, never-ending search for the puzzling, often ambiguous, and yet necessary truth.

We human beings are driven forward by a long and continuous "I don't know." It's not the known that pushes and pulls us along, although we must be serious about preparation, work, discipline, study, and labor. We must also make room to ask the next question, and the next: Why? How does it work? What does it mean? Who benefits and who suffers? What more?

We struggle toward consciousness knowing that being conscious can never be *fully* conscious—we are all more or less conscious, contingently aware, and, at the same time, entirely incomplete. In an infinite and expanding universe, we recognize that our very finiteness means that whatever we know is a tiny fraction of what there is to know, and that our ignorance outweighs our erudition or awareness by a factor of a zillion. This can provoke people to seek out easy answers and available dogma, but it might also lead us to approach others as the active knowledge-creators and meaning-makers that they actually are, as agents in and experts on their own lives. We can approach ourselves as works in progress, too, both incomplete and provisional and on the move.

My friend the cultural worker Lisa Lee likes to chop "truth" up, to shred the word in order to display its complexity. There is, she explains, an element of truth that we might call "forensic truth": this cup of coffee on this countertop is viable and verifiable. But that's not the end of truth's possibilities: there is, as well, individual "narrative truth"—this is the best cup of coffee ever, I made it myself with subtle artistry and served it up with love. And still there's more: another dimension might be thought of as "dialogic truth" as I argue back and forth with Lisa and other friends about the merits of this particular cup, and then bring into view the farmers who grew the beans, the workers who harvested them, and others who transported them down the steep trails and across the seas, the roasters and the truckers and the marketers; we might note the recent clashes between the landlords and the peasants who were forming a farm-workers union, or the Starbucks workers and their exciting union drives. Dialogic truth: the realm of history and culture and politics. We might then consider "restorative truth," or the kinds of things that might be involved in recognizing and accounting for all the labor as well as the many dimensions of meaning-making worked up in this humble cup of joe.

This final dimension of truth—restorative truth—can't be captured in a bullet point. It invites new learning, deeper understanding, vitalized consciousness, and reconciliation. Restorative truth is muscular and hopeful, but it is not the end of anything either. There will always be more work to do.

⸻

Haitian anthropologist Michel-Rolph Trouillot explains that historical truth is both the story of *what happened*—the facts on the ground—as well as the human interpretations and meaning-making perspectives that frame and circulate those grounded facts, or *that which is said to have happened*. People are, then, actors in history and narrators of history—subjects and interpreters, both.[15]

Here's a telling example: fact and story. Robert E. Lee surrendered at the Appomattox Court House in 1865—a fact—but the narrative about the noble Confederate Lost Cause dominated the story about the war for a century and endures to this day. That narrative holds that the foundation of the Confederacy during the American Civil War was just and heroic, defending both the "Southern way of life" and "states' rights" in the face of overwhelming and unjust "Northern aggression." The North won the war while, in several ways and many places, the South won the war to explain the war.

Another example: the Vietnamese won a people's war against French colonialism in the 1950s, survived a decade-long genocidal assault from the US, and emerged victorious and independent. But there are large and powerful voices in the US who insist that the military was "stabbed in the back" by lily-livered politicians—a modern-day Lost Cause.

Or, again: in 1492 a Genoan adventurer in the pay of Castilian royalty stumbled upon the Bahamas (or invaded, conquered, and took the initial steps toward what would become in time the Columbian Holocaust). Hundreds of years later, that act—Columbus's men coming ashore—was made into a narrative, "the discovery of America," and that *naming* created a powerful and abiding frame.

People are agents in that they occupy structural positions (worker, mother, father, farmer); they are also actors in history, moving within the concentric circles of context (economic condition, cultural surround, flow-of-time); and they are subjects (narrators who tell the stories). So, for example, auto workers (agents) in Detroit leave a factory en masse every day; one day they (actors) leave work as UAW members, now withholding their labor to force negotiations with the bosses; they (narrators) call it a strike, and leaving the factory has a different meaning altogether, and the critical fight to control the story is underway.

History is always open to interpretation and reinterpretation—things take on different meanings and shadings and significances as new events unfold. When Chinese premier Zhou Enlai was asked in the early 1960s what he thought the impact of the French revolution of the eighteenth century had been on the twentieth-century Chinese revolution, he responded: "It's too soon to tell." He understood that history is always on the move and in the mix.

Truth and reconciliation are sequential. And there's one more necessary step toward freedom that ties those two together: repair. Without the truth there can be no reconciliation, true, and without repair, the wound will never heal.

A simple example: You accidentally drive through a stoplight and crumple the fender of another car. You admit that it was your fault, and a further responsibility materializes: to repair the damage that you caused to the other car. Saying, "I did it" is a first important, if inadequate, step; next comes repair, and, only then, resolution. That doesn't sound like some wild-eyed radical scheme or some devious socialist plot. It sounds reasonable and fair. Truth and repair and reconciliation.

Here's another example: Your elected city officials hire a contractor who made the lowest bid to do a massive bridge repair. The contractor engages in massive wage theft during the course of the project and then skips town, leaving the city on the hook for a million dollars.

Everyone's taxes go up a few cents in order to compensate the workers and repair the damage. Justice.

When the South African people won their long struggle against colonialism and apartheid, they established the historic Truth and Reconciliation Commission (TRC), arguing that without searching for the truth there could be no authentic freedom and no just future for the country—antagonisms would simply fester, conflict would regroup, and everyone would be barricaded in fear and resentment awaiting the open outbreaks sure to come. Unlike the Nuremberg trials after World War II that sought prosecution and punishment, the TRC encouraged wide public participation and dialogue, seeking accountability for human rights violations and reconciliation between former antagonists. The TRC—imperfect, to be sure—provided a courageous and exciting model for resolving antagonism and conflict on a mass scale. But injustices are rarely repaired, and it's practically axiomatic that the bigger the crime, the less likely the perpetrator will make a good faith effort to repair the harm.

Zora Neale Hurston tells the remarkable story of Kossola, or Cudjo Lewis, the "last 'Black cargo'" in the oral history *Barracoon*.[16] Oluale Kossola was kidnapped in West Africa in 1860, transported to the US, and held as a slave for over five years. Sometime after emancipation and the end of the Civil War, Kossola approached his former owner and explained that without land he and his fellow workers were powerless, and that he felt that the owner owed them something for their unpaid and forced labor. "Cap'n Tim" jumped to his feet and shouted, "Fool do you think I goin' give you property on top of property?" He insisted that he'd always treated "his" slaves well, and that he was the one with the larger grievance—his property (slaves) had been taken, and he was the one deserving compensation.

In *Freedom Dreams*, Robin D. G. Kelley reprints a letter dictated by Jourdan Anderson addressed to his former owner, in which he hopes to test the owner's sincerity "by asking you to send us our wages for the time we served you." He adds up the wages with interest, subtracts basic expenses, and calculates that he is owed $11,680. "We trust the good Maker has opened your eyes to the wrongs which you and your fathers have done to me and my fathers," he continues, "in making us toil for you for generations without recompense."[17] Jourdan Anderson, predictably, got no response.

Before the Emancipation Proclamation, President Abraham Lincoln signed a bill on April 16, 1862, emancipating enslaved people in Washington, DC. Lincoln thought the slaveowners should be compensated for the loss of their property, and the District of Columbia paid those loyal to the Union up to three hundred dollars for every enslaved person freed. Slaveowners got reparations; formerly enslaved African Americans got nothing for their generations of unpaid and forced labor.

In January 1865, General William Tecumseh Sherman met in Savannah, Georgia, with twenty Black ministers, nine of whom had been enslaved workers themselves, who told him unequivocally that what the freed people wanted and needed most was land of their own in order to work their way out of slavery. A few days later, Sherman issued Special Order 15, stipulating the seizure of four hundred thousand acres of land from the traitorous slavers, and the distribution of up to forty acres of land to each formerly enslaved family. The promised "forty acres and a mule," the means of production to allow the formerly enslaved workers to start an independent economic life after the war, were never paid.

As rituals of truth-telling, repair and reconciliation are ancient practices, encoded in law and enacted in major faith traditions: fast, pray, confess, pay tribute, repent. We have a long way to go in the US if we are to achieve repair and even tentatively approach reconciliation.

Embracing freedom also means welcoming humanism: the idea that human life is indeterminate, expansive, and interconnected, that there exists a special human capacity for making history and making meaning, for constructing cultures of connection, for knowledge of who and what we are in the world. Humanism embraces all the things humans make through our own creative thought and labor, including history as an ongoing human construction, and all other forms of expression as well: language and religion and every manner of goods and works and products. Every humanist is drawn—in the spirit of cooperation, sharing, and being-in-common—to explore and expand, to invite the input and engagement of all, and there is no obvious conflict between the practice of humanism and the pursuit of freedom—each unleashes an energy toward enlightenment and liberation.

All of this requires a leaning outward, a willingness to look at the peopled world, at the sufferings, the accomplishments, the perspectives, and the concerns of others, at their twisty, dynamic movement through time, and an awareness—sometimes joyous, but just as often painful—of all that one finds. It requires, as well, a leaning inward toward self-knowledge, a sense of being alive and conscious and growing and changing in a going world.

In each direction we acknowledge that every person is entangled and propelled, and sometimes made mute, by a social surround, that each also has a wild and vast inner life; each has a story to tell, meanings to make and remake. We inhabit an infinite and dynamic world, a world in motion, and we are ourselves unfinished, unruly sparks of meaning-making energy on a voyage of discovery and surprise. History, as always, charges relentlessly forward, and the world, as always, is in process. Going inward without consciously connecting to a larger world leads to self-referencing and, worse, narcissism as truth; traveling outward without noting your own embodied heart and mind can lead to ethical near-sightedness, seeing other three-dimensional human beings as cardboard cutouts, monochromatic background to your own colorful life. The powerful assume they have agency, history, culture—they write the rest of us off by our statistical profiles. Resist joining that particular inhumane habit of the powerful.

What are the challenges to human beings today? What does the hope for democracy demand of us now? Edward Said points out that the US incorporates "fantastic resources and accomplishments, but it also contains a redoubtable set of internal inequities and external interventions that cannot be ignored."[18] We are faced with the enduring stain of white supremacy and the ever more elusive and intractable barriers to racial justice, the enthronement of greed, and the rapidly widening gulf between the obscenely rich, working people, and the poor. We are faced as well with aggressive economic and military adventures abroad, the macho posturing of men bonding in groups and enacting a kind of theatrical but no less real militarism, the violence of conquest and occupation from Palestine and Central Asia to South America and our own urban centers.

Encountering these facts thrusts us into the realm of human agency and choice, the battlefield of social action and change, where we come face to face with several stubborn questions: Can we stop the suffering? Can we alleviate at least some of the pain? Can we repair any of the loss? There are deeper considerations, too: Can society be changed at all? Is it remotely possible (not inevitable, certainly) for people to come together freely, to imagine a more just and peaceful social order, to join hands and organize for something better—for freedom—and to win? Can we do anything?

Freedom lovers can be humanists without becoming anthropocentric, for humanism doesn't mean human triumphalism, the domination and exploitation of the vast world with its brilliant dance of living things and the Earth itself. We know that the planet will go on in some form for millions and millions of years; we would also like the Earth, our planet and our only home, to be a place fit for all. Living in harmony with—indeed, in awe of—this unique home planet is the only way to live fully, abundantly, and to survive.

The humanist ambition is for every human being to reach the fullest measure of their own humanity. Freedom. This leads necessarily to raucous and participatory pursuits—open to every background and class and condition in its perpetual asking of new questions, its continual discoveries, its ceaseless and essential reformulations and revisions and unique revelations.

We recognize that every human being, no matter who, is a gooey biological wonder, pulsing with the breath and beat of life itself, eating, sleeping, pissing and shitting, prodded by sexual urges, evolved and evolving, shaped by genetics, twisted and gnarled and hammered by the unique experiences of living. I'll echo Eugene V. Debs, the American labor organizer and freedom fighter: "I am kin to all that throbs."[19]

Every human being also has a unique and complex set of circumstances that makes their life understandable and sensible, bearable or unbearable. This recognition asks us to reject any action that treats anyone as an object, any gesture that *thingifies* others. It demands that we embrace every human being, and that we take their side.

If a fairer, saner, and more just society is both desirable and possible, if we can imagine and build together a public space for the enactment of our freedom dreams, the field opens slightly. There would still be much to be done, for nothing would be entirely settled. We would still need to find ways to stir ourselves from passivity, cynicism, and despair, to reach beyond the superficial barriers that wall us off from one another, to resist the flattening social evils like institutionalized racism, to shake off the anesthetizing impact of the authoritative, official voices that dominate so much of our space, to release our imaginations and to act on behalf of what the known demands, linking our conduct firmly to our consciousness. We would have to launch ourselves once more into the never-ending search for truth, repair, reconciliation, and freedom.

6

STUDYING FREEDOM/
TEACHING ABOLITION

**"WOKE UP THIS MORNING WITH
MY MIND STAYED ON FREEDOM"**

*Woke up this morning with my mind
stayed on freedom.
Woke up this morning with my mind
stayed on freedom.
Woke up this morning with my mind
stayed on freedom*

*Hallelu (hallelu)
Hallelu (hallelu)
Hallelujah*

*I'm walking and talking with my mind
stayed on freedom.
Walking and talking with my mind
stayed on freedom.
(You know I'm) walking and talking with my mind
stayed on freedom.
Hallelu (hallelu)
Hallelu (hallelu)
Hallelujah*

—REVEREND ROBERT WESBY

With our minds stayed on freedom, we take a two-eyed approach to life: one eye focused intently on the world as such, here and now—the wild, lovely, damaged, dynamic, true world we inhabit; the other eye squinting as it searches the far horizon for a possible world—a future more balanced, more just, and more free than anything we've ever known. We reject the logic of prisons with all its accompanying

(continued)

constraints and limits, imposed restrictions, and forced impediments that pass as common sense. We seek knowledge, wide-awakeness, and a vision of freedom itself—vast and alive, churning and changing, rising and falling, something we can move toward and aspire to as we make our wobbly ways forward. Create a list of the ways you can show up with your visions of freedom intact and make them practical in your everyday liberatory practice.

— REFLECTION SIX: TEACH FREEDOM —

"I shall create!" a juvenile delinquent cries out in Gwendolyn Brooks's poem "Boy Breaking Glass," and the words, coming from the mouth of this imagined "bad boy," land with particular power and poignancy. "If not a note, a hole," he continues. "If not an overture, a desecration."[1] No matter what you've been told, and no matter what the pundits and talking heads have insistently professed about this boy, Brooks reminds us that his urgent intent is universal: *I shall create.*

How shall we respond to the dreams of youth? How shall we answer that heartfelt cry, the elemental human aspiration to leave a footprint in the sand? How will we hear the authentic voices of people—especially the marginalized, the outcast, those deemed disposable by the powerful, or considered "the leastwise of the land"—above the steady roar of commentary about them?

We've considered freedom from several angles of regard, its challenges and its demands, its contradictions and paradoxes, and we've asked in context after context, how do we get free? I'll turn to the classroom now, a space where teachers and students come together formally and routinely to teach and to learn. Each time I use the word *teacher*, however, you might add a mental parenthesis, and insert an appropriate synonym: union or community organizer, activist, artist, social justice movement-maker. The practice of good teaching and the work of participatory democracy are in broad strokes the same thing.

We recognize that in all times and all places, institutions—schools, courts, police forces, punishment bureaucracies, media, military—are built to serve a specific social structure. Their first and primary purpose is tied to the existing order, a particular economic/political/social system, and a dominant class. And so if we know, for example, that the old South Africa was an apartheid society, we could be fairly certain that the media and the police were designed to enforce and reinforce that system, that the schools would necessarily be strictly segregated by race, that privileges would be distributed along the color line, and that the curriculum would justify a white supremacist ideology and promote the racial hierarchy. Conversely, if you looked at the schools, the courts, or the jails, you would be able to reckon with some precision what the system of apartheid must be like in every other institution, and in the larger society.

In a theocracy, whatever else is taught in the schools and practiced in the larger society, faithful obedience to God's representatives would be central—people are taught to genuflect as a sign of deference and can be punished for violating their religious teachings; in a kingdom, fealty to the royals is dominant and enforced; and in a dictatorship, obedience and conformity are the most essential lessons, taught repeatedly alongside language and math and science. But it's worth noting that medieval Saudi Arabia, fascist Italy, and Nazi Germany produced brilliant scientists, great artists, fine athletes, and prosperity for some, while at the same time producing large numbers of people who would follow orders unthinkingly straight to the gates of hell.

Imagine what an outsider might deduce about US society after visiting a classroom in wealthy suburban Winnetka, and then another on the West Side of Chicago. They would surely note that schools reproduce the existing social relations—advantage and disadvantage organized along traditional race and class and gender categories—and they might see as well that the schools can be, and often are, sites of conflict and contention.

Institutions in a free society—even a society with mere aspirations toward freedom—would follow a path with a distinct set of values designed specifically for free people. Initiative and courage would be applauded; imagination and creativity nourished; nonconformity and noncompliance respected; ingenuity and enterprise nurtured; dissent

and disagreement encouraged; and diversity and dissimilarity celebrated. Those are the hallmarks of free people.

Teachers and movement-makers in a free society would demon-
strate through words and actions that, whoever you are and wherever
you're from, you have every right to be here, and you should expect
and demand, therefore, to be treated with compassion, respect, and
camaraderie. Enlightenment and liberation are your birthrights, and
you deserve to live a life of love, joy, purpose, and solidarity. You also
have huge reserves of potential and more promise and agency than
are typically acknowledged; these ought to be recognized fully and
nourished through regular exercise. And—there's more, but let's underline this point because book-burning is back in style, the thought
police are on the rise, and the Salem witch trials aren't so very long
ago after all—you need no one's permission to interrogate the world.
Read everything, talk to everyone, get into conversation with the wid-
est possible overlapping circles of people, and break all the rules and
taboos that would curb your curiosity and your right to know. If you are
in fact free, then *you need no one's permission to interrogate the world!*

In 2023, Florida's reactionary governor Ron DeSantis published
The Courage to Be Free, subtitled "Florida's Blueprint for America's
Revival," a faux memoir that doubles as the *Mein Kampf* of an am-
bitious politician aching to be seen as both serious and human.[2] For
DeSantis, freedom, in the Florida blueprint, insists that Floridians
(and Americans) explicitly do not interrogate the world. The Florida
state legislature passed a bill in 2022 called the Individual Freedom
Act, initially known as the Stop WOKE Act—Wrongs to Our Kids
and Employees. The turning of "woke" into a watchword is itself an
anti-Black gesture—the term has long been used in Black English to
denote being aware, being deeply conscious. "Woke" entered political
discourse meaning being attuned to Black insights and Black sensibilities on issues; the backlash against the term is an act of linguistic
lynching.

Notice the use of the contested word "freedom" in the title of the
bill and in DeSantis's book, and note further that the bill outlaws
classroom discussion of sexual orientation through grade three, rejects

math textbooks that don't meet an opaque review process, forbids the teaching of this country's history of racism, and bans discussion of racial or gender privilege or oppression if there's a chance it might cause someone "discomfort, guilt, anguish or any other form of psychological distress."[3] Unfreedom! This is white fragility enshrined, and the thought police rising! The book burning could begin with anything written by the Reverend Martin Luther King Jr., including his sermons ("America Is Going to Hell"), speeches ("Beyond Vietnam"), and his books (*Where Do We Go from Here? Chaos or Community*).

One of the objectionable texts in Florida is David Walker's *Appeal to the Colored Citizens of the World*, a withering attack on slavery and US hypocrisy published in 1829.[4] The appeal was immediately banned in every slave state and quickly led to legislation prohibiting teaching reading to enslaved workers. When Frederick Douglass's master discovered that his wife was teaching the enslaved Douglass to read, he exploded in anger and shouted, "It will unfit him to be a slave!"[5] Exactly, and perfectly symmetrical with today's racially fired bans.

Several teachers brought suit in Florida, calling the Stop WOKE Act "racially motivated censorship" intended to stifle widespread demands to "discuss, study, and address systemic inequalities." A federal judge ruled that Florida cannot "choose which viewpoints are worthy of illumination and which must remain in the shadows," or "impose its own orthodoxy."[6] The judge's ruling began by quoting the opening line from George Orwell's *1984*: "It was a cold day in April, and the clocks were striking thirteen."[7] He continued, "And the powers in charge of Florida's public university system have declared the State has unfettered authority to muzzle its professors in the name of 'freedom.' This is positively dystopian."[8]

This is far from the end of the fight. Former secretary of state Mike Pompeo recently called the head of the American Federation of Teachers "the most dangerous person in the world" and noted that "if our kids don't grow up understanding America is an exceptional nation, we're done. If they think it's an oppressor class and an oppressed class, if they think . . . we were founded on a racist idea . . . it's difficult to understand how Xi Jinping's claim that America is in decline won't prove true."[9] I just sent both Ron DeSantis and Mike Pompeo copies of James Allen's *Without Sanctuary* (2000), an archive of twentieth-century lynching photographs, many with victims surrounded by crowds of white people smiling and posing for the cameras. An exceptional nation indeed.

In David Diop's bracing novel *At Night All Blood Is Black*, the narrator says, "No one knows what I think. I am free to think whatever I want. And what I think is that people don't want me to think."[10] Diop brings to mind James Baldwin's classic 1963 "A Talk to Teachers":

> The purpose of education, finally, is to create in a person the ability to look at the world for himself, to make his own decisions, to say to himself this is black or this is white, to decide for himself whether there is a God in heaven or not. To ask questions of the universe, and then learn to live with those questions, is the way he achieves his own identity. But no society is really anxious to have that kind of person around. What societies really, ideally, want is a citizenry which will simply obey the rules of society. If a society succeeds in this, that society is about to perish. The obligation of anyone who thinks of himself as responsible is to examine society and try to change it and to fight it—at no matter what risk. This is the only hope society has.[11]

We are asked to pass on the received wisdom of this time and this place, to reproduce the society as it is. But a responsible teacher—parent, organizer, freedom fighter, abolitionist, artist, writer, journalist, citizen, resident—must refuse to lie and might create in students, then, the temperament to discover and question the world. That means not only acknowledging genocide and slavery but also looking deeply at the present; it means rejecting the clichéd and commonsense framings or explanations of things and going to the root. For example, a liberal reading of the contemporary issues of poverty, welfare, food stamps, housing for the homeless, and the crisis of immigration and refugees might lead to sympathetic support for people facing these challenges. But this fails the test of complete honesty because it flatlines before getting to the root.

It's one thing to struggle for housing for the unhoused (motel accommodations, tiny houses, shelters) and quite another thing to dive more deeply into questions concerning massive income inequality, tax codes, redlining, wage theft, and other structural realities that drove people out of homes and into the streets. Welfare payments to workers who are not able to cover expenses—OK—but we can also investigate and research the problem of subsidizing sub-survival wages paid by bosses. And we can resist. Building survival camps for refugees arriving at the border, leaving food and water in the desert, and advocating for immigrants in court are surely decent and humane acts, but we can go further and deeper if we name the reality that deporting refugees is a form of ethnic cleansing, and that people are fleeing wars created by our government, fleeing, as well, environmental collapse and economic crises caused by an imperial economy of extraction. Refugees in America and Europe are, in Juan Gonzalez's illuminating phrase, the "harvest of empire."[12]

We study freedom when we tell the truth and create the conditions for expanding participation and popular power—and when we take agency as a universal human endowment and an essential energy to unleash. Self-education is consequential, then, precisely because it requires and represents the exercise of agency. Not only do you not require authorization to examine and critically question society, you also don't need someone else's reading list to get started. And, of course, you don't need an official endorsement to link arms with others in order to change whatever needs changing. We study freedom when we foreground the arts of liberty: imagination, creativity, initiative, courage, risk-taking.

I mentioned earlier Emily Dickinson's lovely picture of the imagination igniting the "slow fuse of possibility." I can see in my mind's eye the fuse cracking and sparkling toward what could be but is not yet, the eyes opening wide, followed by the hand striking the match.[13] We study freedom when we light it up.

Gwendolyn Brooks asked, "Does man love art?" Her answer, "Man visits Art but squirms. / Art hurts. Art urges voyages."[14] The voyages art demands lie at the very heart of freedom: journeys in search of new solutions to old problems, explorations of spirit spaces and emotional landscapes, trips into the hidden meanings and elaborate schemes we construct to make our lives understandable and endurable, flights hooked on metaphor and analogy, wobbly rambles away from the cold reality of the world we inhabit—the world as such—into worlds that could be or should be standing just beyond the far horizon. These voyages emphasize the capacities and features that mark us as uniquely human: aspiration, self-awareness, projection, desire, ingenuity, compassion, and commitment—all of these and more are harvests of our imaginations.

But it's also true that art hurts. The capacity to see the world as if it could be otherwise creates yearning and liberates desire—we are freed (or condemned) to run riot. Imagination—necessarily subversive, unruly, and disruptive—challenges the status quo simply by opening us up to consider alternatives. Art makes the familiar strange, forcing us to look at things in new ways. Suddenly the taken-for-granted and the given world become choices and no longer warrants or life (death?) sentences.

Before we go further, I once more call forth my brilliant teacher Maxine Greene's warning that it takes a fierce and dangerous imagination to summon the Guantanamo Bay US military prison in Cuba or the brutal American prison complex Abu Ghraib in Iraq or the "tiger cages," pit-like concrete boxes built below ground by the French colonialists and utilized by the US military on Con Son Island, Vietnam. Don't romanticize or idealize the "imagination," she advised, but work to encourage and unleash the *social* imagination, the collectively creative, inventive, resourceful forces that embrace all of humanity and are explicitly pro-emancipation and pro-liberation for the many, for all.

We study freedom when we acknowledge and participate in struggles that attempt to enlarge the realm of popular agency and human rights (Black Freedom, women's liberation, LGBTQI rights, immigrant rights, disabled rights) and campaigns for greater justice (full voting rights, prison abolition, care not cops, demilitarization at home and abroad, universal access to excellent education). We study freedom when we develop a curriculum of problem-posing and question-asking, and a pedagogy grounded in dialogue in which the teacher assumes as a fundamental responsibility the work of unlocking the wisdom in the room. Our overriding assumption is that education is a human right, and that teaching is complex intellectual and ethical work requiring a thoughtful and caring person at its heart.

We also study freedom when we organize groups for serious and sustained inquiry and investigation. My study group has recently watched and listened to several documentaries together in order to think more clearly about the requirements of movement-building: *Crip Camp, The Black Panther Party: Vanguard of the Revolution, The Janes, Time, Bus Riders Union, Mother Country Radicals, Free Chol Soo Lee*. We've read and studied contemporary pieces by Barbara Ransby, Keeanga-Yamahtta Taylor, Robin D. G. Kelley, Roxanne Dunbar-Ortiz, Angela Davis, Mariame Kaba, Beth Richie, Erica Meiners, Nikole Hannah Jones, Gina Dent, and Ta-Nehisi Coates, as well as classics from W. E. B. Du Bois, Franz Fanon, Grace Lee and Jimmy Boggs, Karl Marx, Rosa Luxembourg, and James Baldwin. In one recent illuminating gathering, we read and studied together the 1964 Mississippi Freedom School curriculum, the Combahee River Collective statement, the Black Panther Party Ten-Point Program, and the First Declaration of the Lacandon Jungle issued by the Zapatistas in Chiapas, Mexico.

Here is a powerful example of studying freedom and teaching abolition, a classic American story I turn to repeatedly for inspiration and enlightenment.

In 1963, Charlie Cobb, a young field secretary with the Student Nonviolent Coordinating Committee (SNCC), the militant young people who led the freedom rides and lunch-counter sit-ins, wrote a brief proposal to create a number of Freedom Schools throughout Mississippi in order to revitalize the Civil Rights Movement. While the Black youth of the South, he argued, were denied many things—decent school facilities, honest and forward-looking curriculum, fully qualified teachers—the fundamental injury was "a complete absence of academic freedom and students are forced to live in an environment that is geared to squashing intellectual curiosity, and different thinking." He called the classrooms of Mississippi "intellectual wastelands," and he challenged himself and others "to fill an intellectual and creative vacuum in the lives of young Negro Mississippi, and to get them to articulate their own desires, demands and questions."[15] Their own desires, their own demands, and their own questions—for African Americans living in semifeudal bondage and the afterlife of slavery, managed and contained through a system of law and custom as well as outright terror, this was a revolutionary proposal indeed, a giant leap of the radical imagination, and at the same time so completely characteristic of the Black Freedom Movement.

Andrew Goodman, James Chaney, and Mickey Schwerner were all SNCC volunteers engaged in the Freedom Schools. They had been investigating the arson bombing of a church that hosted one of the schools when they were arrested and jailed in June 1964; they were released into the dark of night, and then kidnapped and brutally lynched near Philadelphia, Mississippi, by the Ku Klux Klan, with the police acting as enablers and partners. The revolutionary meaning of the Freedom Schools wasn't lost on the rulers of Mississippi—their power and potential was understood well by the barbarians and their terrorist enforcers.

The world-shaking significance of the Freedom Schools—their prospects, legacy, and cost—should not be lost on us either. The Freedom Schools were fugitive institutions teaching contraband curriculum and Black history, and introducing students to concepts of popular education and community research. "We're investigating and interrogating the world," they announced. Freedom Libraries sprung up, new ideas took shape everywhere, windows were thrown open, and fresh winds were allowed to blow.[16] This is legacy, and this, too, was met with fear and violence as Freedom Libraries were torched and civil rights workers attacked and arrested. Today, Tracie D. Hall, the current and first African American executive director of the American Library Association, is a fierce and persistent opponent of book banning in any form; she has also made it a priority to build and strengthen libraries everywhere, starting with building robust libraries in every prison in the land. Her work today is guided by a phrase that has become her fiery motto: "Free People Read Freely."

Let's revisit Charlie Cobb's premise for today, focusing on the young folks who've been written off and marginalized by the powerful and mainstream society. They are First Nations people or the descendants of formerly enslaved and African-ancestored people or recent immigrants from poor countries. They're from working-class families—people who survive by selling their labor power, and even then frequently in the informal economy. They've attended schools of poverty, and many have participated in a sort of general strike and run away from those schools. They have endured institutions (not only schools but also police forces and La Migra, courts and hospitals) that routinely refuse to recognize them, disregarding their humanity and denying their full personhood. The youth of South Central Los Angeles or Detroit or Philadelphia or New Orleans or the West Side of Chicago are denied many things, but the fundamental injury is a complete absence of academic freedom. Students are "forced to live in an environment that is geared to squashing intellectual curiosity and different thinking." What would it mean and how would it look if they were to mobilize themselves in order to articulate their own desires, their own demands and dreams, their own questions? I think the world would crack open—as it did in Mississippi—in the best possible way.

Because our radical social imaginations are tenacious, they doggedly refuse to go quietly into that dark, dark night. When significant numbers of people are encouraged to pursue their curiosity and passion, when another world seems not only desirable to a large enough group but also possible, the status quo becomes suddenly and surprisingly unbearable, and revolution is in the air.

Black people in Mississippi knew that the Jim Crow system was unjust and cruel from the start; that was not news to them, for they'd lived it, suffered its lash, and stood up where they could. They had expressed their agency and resisted their oppression in a thousand clandestine ways (foot-dragging, absenteeism, sabotage) when they lacked the luxury of open politics. And there were thousands of individual acts of open defiance—on trains and on public buses, for example—that continually pushed the limits of what was possible. But when people collectively got the notion in their minds that if they risked, for instance, registering to vote (a life-and-death proposition, an invitation to beatings and chain gangs), a more just world could be pried open for them and their children, and, indeed, for their entire community, the risk was taken, the battle engaged, and a wall was breached releasing an irresistible tide—freedom! There's no sound so sweet as the sound of chains that had held folks back for so long falling noisily to the ground. And it's still true: once we can reimagine and resist in significant numbers, we will rise again, reaching for new heights and setting better foundations for living and loving, for building a new community and a better world.

The Mississippi Freedom School curriculum was organized around questions: Why are you and I in the Freedom Movement? What do we hope to accomplish? What would we like to change? The whole idea was to summon people to name the circumstances of their own lives, to encourage them to a serious consideration of how those circumstances might be changed, and to invite them into a space of authentic democracy and participatory action. This was studying freedom and teaching abolition: abolition of Jim Crow, abolition of racial segregation, abolition of white supremacy.

What do we hope to accomplish? What will help us realize our deepest dreams and desires? In what ways is education liberating, and in what ways can schooling be entangling and oppressive? Can learning be cast as a creative act, enjoyable and social, or must it always be framed as competitive and brutal? What does it mean to be an educated person? What does it mean to be free? Awakened to fundamental and forbidden questions, a new world of possibilities comes into view.

In the Mississippi Freedom Schools, student experiences and student insights were a driving force in all the matters students and teachers inquired into and all the projects they undertook. Education was linked to life. No longer an abstraction, education became a vital matter of organizing toward community empowerment and collective freedom. The main pedagogical gesture in Freedom Schools was dialogue: speaking with the possibility of being heard and listening with the expectation of being transformed in some large or small measure. They offered experiences with debate and discussion, experiments in associative living, exercises in learning to live together, and a rich culture of recognition combined with a profound compassion for one another and our shared world.

In one class, SNCC field secretary Stokely Carmichael wrote pairs of sentences on the board next to one another: "I digs wine" and "I enjoy cocktails"; "I be's unhappy" and "I am dissatisfied." He provoked a propulsive conversation about the power of language as a means of communication as well as a signifier of social position. The students walked away conscious of the codes of power and some of the invisible threads of oppression, as well as with a stronger sense of their own capacity to name and change the world.

Students and teachers were set up to learn *from* the world, not about it; *from* fish and farming, construction and carpentry, gardening, history, and quantum mechanics—not simply about them. Freedom School classes studied voting patterns, property values, and health problems in the community. One class conducted a countywide survey of land ownership and made a chart tracing patterns of wealth transfer back to slavery. This is teaching freedom. All of the classes were organized around learning by doing: interrogating, acting, producing, inquiring, and participating. No longer a set of anemic destinations, learning went deeper and traveled further. And, most important, students developed confidence in themselves as creators and meaning-makers in an infinite universe, not simply consumers of a static and unjust world. They were learning freedom, and they were also *practicing* freedom.

At the same time as the Freedom Schools were being built, Paolo Freire, a continent away, was developing the same curriculum in Brazil, again propelled by a social movement and the demands of the times. Freire also argued that students must have the right to interrogate the world, not just to decode the word. And he proposed that students and teachers together explore common problems and work together to solve them. This was education as freedom, school as revolution, and part of the anticolonial uprisings that spread throughout the Third World.

Freire's method was not to bestow wisdom, even radical wisdom, from above—it was not a new dogma of settled truths. Instead, Freire pursued revolution in the pedagogy itself, in the way classes were conducted. The wisdom, desires, insights, and direction of the students themselves was the center of the curriculum and the teaching. Students were reading the world while they were reading the word.

Imagine a "citizenship curriculum" inviting research, reading, writing, deep study, dialogue, and debate around a revised set of questions for this moment:

What are schools for? Who decides? What do people learn in school? What should they learn? Where else do we learn?

Are all public schools the same? What are the differences? Where do the differences come from? Who decides? What is the cost of education? How are schools funded? Are schools funded fairly? How do you know?

What is academic success? Who decides? What is standardized testing? Is it fair? How do you know? How big is the testing business? Has it always been this way? Who profits?

How many prisons are there in Mississippi? In Illinois? Who does time, and for what crimes? How much money goes into incarceration, and how much into education? Who decides? Where is the nearest prison or jail? Are people who are in prison allowed to read widely or to interrogate the world? Why not? Can incarcerated people vote? Why not?

What youth gangs exist in our community? What appeals to kids about gangs? What are some things that gangs offer that are positive? What things are destructive and harmful to participants, to the larger community?

What makes you an American? Who decides? If someone questioned your right to call yourself an American, what story would you offer as proof? What image or object would you produce that could be persuasive?

Once started it's hard to stop asking questions—one thing leads to another in an endless trail. And once we take a first step onto this path, we begin to recognize that power is hidden in every question, and that everything is connected to everything else if we pursue it deeply enough.

I went with a group of third-graders at a small public elementary school in Chicago on a trip to Lake Michigan recently. One of them asked, "Who owns the water?" and speculation included Donald Trump, Elon Musk, Oprah Winfrey, and the police. The teacher who pursued this question with her eight- and nine-year-old students led an exploration of discovery and surprise that swept into areas of pollution and environmental science, the meaning of water in Chicago versus Chiapas, the role of water in civilization, the art and poetry of water.

Let's go further, imagining what schools and classrooms could become if empathy, care, compassion, and solidarity were the order of the day, and if freedom, liberation, and abolition were not only the current of curriculum and instruction but also the presiding cultural touchstone.

Education for free people is powered by a precious and fragile ideal: every human being is of infinite and incalculable value, each a work in progress and a force in motion, a unique intellectual, emotional, physical, spiritual, moral, and creative force; each endowed with reason and conscience and agency; each deserving a dedicated place in a community of solidarity as well as a vital sense of brotherhood and sisterhood, recognition and respect. This means that the fullest development of each individual—given the tremendous range of ability and the delicious stew of race, ethnicity, points of origin, and backgrounds—is the necessary condition for the full development of the entire community and, conversely, that the fullest development of all is essential for the full development of each.

The Reverend Martin Luther King Jr. said, "I can never be what I ought to be until you are what you ought to be. You can never be what you ought to be until I am what I ought to be."[17] For him this was the "inescapable network of mutuality" and the "single garment of destiny."

To be ruled is to be spied upon and summed up, inspected, regulated, and indoctrinated, registered and admonished, corrected and measured, tested and ranked, with all the inherent structural violence packed into those arrangements, and to be free is to abolish that system, to reject its hold over our minds as well as its power in the world. If our minds are set on freedom, we must experience freedom ourselves, and we must teach free people to be free. While schools are rightly indicted for reproducing racial and patriarchal hierarchies, they are also sites of contention and struggle, one of the only institutions of society in which every day we confront, potentially, the big questions, like: What kind of society do we want to live in? What world will we build?

The relationship between education and freedom is deep, intrinsic, and profound—each is concerned with the fullest expression of human development. To the extent that people reflect upon their lives and become more conscious of themselves as actors in the world, conscious, too, of the vast range of alternatives that can be imagined and expressed in any given situation, capable of joining in community and asserting themselves as subjects in history, constructors of the human world, they recreate themselves as free human beings.

Teachers can create classrooms where students with a range of backgrounds, perspectives, experiences, and beliefs learn to live with and for one another. A pedagogy of dialogue—beginning with a question, and then asking the next question, and then the next—is the basic teaching gesture in and for a free people. Learning the fine art of speaking with the possibility of being heard, and listening with the possibility of being changed is a practical contribution to finding one's way in a wildly diverse democracy.

Education is a fundamental human right and a basic community responsibility. Every child, simply by being born, has the right to a free, accessible, high-quality public education. That means that a decent, generously staffed school facility must be in easy reach for every family. This is not at all difficult to envision: what the most privileged parents have for their children right now—small class sizes, fully trained and well-compensated teachers, physics and chemistry labs, sports teams, physical education, and athletic fields and gymnasiums, afterschool and summer programs, generous arts programs that include music, theater, and fine arts—is the baseline for what we want for all the children of our communities. Anything less weakens and then destroys democracy.

If freedom is the horizon, we need to abolish schools that are hauling the dead weight of brute competition, monstrous individualism, and the legacy of white supremacy on their broken backs. We might find ways to create and nourish freedom schools in every town and village, every community and neighborhood—standing tall, arm-in-arm freedom-schoolers might hammer out a call for "Free Schools for Free People."

We can easily imagine popular assemblies shaped from the grassy grassroots and mobilized to build a bold, creative, and spirited mass movement—a red-hot fire from below—to demand the schools we need and the schools we deserve. These assemblies could focus on fundamental questions: Who are we? Where do we come from? What does this time require of us now? Where do we want to go? In our dream of dreams, what should a good school look like in a free and democratic society? What do schools need to do in order to fulfill the needs of free people committed to mutual aid and community health? What could schools be, and what should they become, as fundamental pillars of a free society? Dare the schools build a free social order? These audacious gatherings might be guided by a bold motto: "Be realistic—demand the impossible!"

Imagine generating a (draft) ten-point program:

1. Education is a basic human right and a fundamental freedom—it cannot be reduced to a product to be sold at the marketplace. **We demand** generous, full, and equitable funding for public schools, and not another penny of public money used to advance the potent but deeply corrupt campaign to privatize public education.

2. Education is freedom. Given the harsh, unresolved history of white supremacy, and the adaptable and slippery nature of racial capitalism, it's no surprise that the descendants of enslaved workers, African-ancestored youth, the children of First Nations people and the laboring classes and immigrants from formerly colonized nations too often experience schooling as oppressive and colonizing rather than liberating. The public schools can and must become sites of resistance, vigorously combatting institutional racism, racial discrimination, segregation, and all forms of oppression. Black and Brown and Indigenous students deserve reparations for centuries of prison-like schools. **We demand** an end to racism and white supremacy in both policy and curriculum, the termination of zero-tolerance policies, the abolition of police in our schools, and the elimination of the well-documented school-to-prison pipeline.

3. Education for free people stands firmly on two legs: knowledge and liberation. **We demand** curriculum and teaching that allow young people to imagine and construct the kind of economy and society in which they can thrive, a social order that foregrounds not obedience and conformity but rather the arts of liberty—respect for oneself and others, initiative and courage, imagination and curiosity, problem-posing and problem-solving, mutual aid and solidarity—which are essential to a free people.

4. Education must allow each person to reach the fullest measure of their promise and potential. In a strong democracy the full development of each is the condition for the full development of all, and, conversely, the full development all is the condition for the fullest development of each. **We demand** an end to the massively expensive high-stakes, standardized testing regime and its obsession with sorting "winners" from "losers," which only serves to exacerbate existing racial, social, and educational inequities.

5. Education, like life and like art, begins in wonder. Learning to construct and create, to question and to experiment, to

imagine and interrogate, to wonder and to wander—this is the work of the arts as well as the sturdiest foundation upon which to build an education of purpose for a free people. **We demand** a full arts program in every school.

6. Education is embedded in community, and schools belong to and must serve the real material and cultural needs and aspirations of those communities. **We demand** safe and secure high-quality public schools—community schools and afterschool programs for all children, universal child-centered early childhood programs, nurses and counselors on-site, and free universal school meals—centers of community health and education embedded in safe communities, without regard to wealth or location.

7. Education builds on relationships, and sustainable relationships are difficult to achieve in large, impersonal factory-type schools. **We demand** smaller class size and smaller schools.

8. Education depends on thoughtful, caring people in every classroom performing the essential ethical and intellectual work of teaching, and good schools build on the collective wisdom of teachers and staff in conversation with one another. **We demand** a standard starting salary for teachers of no less than $80,000 annually and expanded collective bargaining rights.

9. Education recognizes that each person is the one of one—sacred, unique, and immeasurably valuable—and, at the same time, each is just one part of the whole human family. **We demand** a curriculum that affirms both our individuality and our collectivity, that acknowledges the ongoing human struggle to achieve equality and justice, and that ensures generous funding for special education.

10. **We demand** a school experience worthy of the dreams of youth.

Authentic education (as opposed to much of what we call schooling) recognizes that everything that counts can't be counted, and that everything that's counted doesn't necessarily count. We want to build schools that recognize children and youth as three-dimensional beings and not a collection of deficits and defects, and that acknowledge explicitly—and make count—the values of love, joy, justice, beauty, kindness, compassion, commitment, curiosity, peace, effort, interest, engagement, awareness, connectedness, happiness, sense of humor, relevance, honesty, self-confidence, and freedom.

Imagine coming together and building schools that prepare free people to participate fully in a free society—schools that young people don't have to recover from. Imagine abolishing schools as they are in order to build freedom schools, each one acting as a hopeful launch pad for the dreams of all youth.

I've taught or cotaught a class called Writing Our Lives in state prison for several years. Our students are all men serving life or de-facto life sentences of thirty years or more. These men are artists, writers, poets, civic leaders, mentors, and lifelong learners, and their written work is the stuff of three-dimensional, complicated human beings, full of humor, sorrow, and longing—for love and freedom, for joy and understanding. They've written lyrical raps, short stories, and essays on transport, migration, gun violence, racism, book banning, learning to dance, exercising, coming of age, and wanting to fit in. Settings have included nightclubs in Mexico City; prisons in Arizona; homes in Muskegon, Michigan; El trains and TV rooms in Chicago. One essay featured the prison barbershop, about which writer and barber Abdul Jabbar wrote, "Staphylococci, Streptococci, Diplococci, Bacilli, and Spirilla are just some of the pathogenic bacteria I must protect you from." These pieces are about protection, fear, and danger. They are about wanting. Moses wrote about wishing, as a kid, that he could just help his mom pay for basic necessities: "So, to help mom out plus go to Cosmo's party and skating, I figured I would sell some weed, buy a fourth (of a pound) and sell all joints—I wanted to buy me: some Herman The Monster shoes, a John Wayne shirt, and some Sergio Valente jeans." The essays are about plans—some gone wrong, others deferred, still more newly imagined. Victor wrote about the night before he left Mexico City for America: "My mother knew that if I was to stay in Mexico, I was either going to get killed by the cartel or by drugs. And alcohol would eventually catch up to me. So Plan 'Z' was for me to go live with my dad." These are about plans from A to Z. Michael wrote about his arrival on the prison bus that the guys called "The Bluebird": "I looked out the window and saw a 30-feet concrete wall hovering over the bus and my unmovable body. The wall appeared to be a domineering fixture, echoing the omnipotent sounds of a group of ghosts." Class was always concerned with living and with ghosts, with our own time and with the countless histories running underneath us.

Teaching and learning can be demanding in any venue or circumstance, but every challenge is magnified and intensified when the classroom is in a prison—the difficulty of negotiating clotted bureaucracies; the struggle of trying to overcome institutional norms that value passivity and obedience; the strain of working under the harsh lights of pervasive surveillance. Teachers and students in a prison classroom cannot communicate outside of class, cannot meet for office hours, cannot appear to be developing friendships or connections that might threaten to strengthen the bonds with the outside world that prison works tirelessly to limit or destroy. Our students agreed early on to summon the better angels of ourselves, and to vitalize generosity, grace, and forgiveness no matter what barriers were thrown at us. There were many: unannounced lockdowns, a student put "on punishment" in solitary confinement, another student transferred without warning to a prison downstate, a sudden staff shortage forcing class cancellation. These disruptive if routine interruptions were components of a culture of mindless authority, arbitrary rules, and the intentional destruction of human connectedness.

Authentic learning requires free thought and categorical permission to interrogate the world. As noted earlier, it is undermined when students are inspected, spied upon, regulated, appraised, censured, measured, registered, counted, admonished, sermonized—or caged and pigeonholed. These are normal conventions behind bars, and so our students created new norms, made spaces where we could speak truthfully, acknowledge our histories and values, and catch glimpses of freedom.

Our students inspired us every day: their commitment to education as a pathway to changing one's life awed us; their insights and interventions reminded us to accept as valid the lived experiences of others; and their struggles to remain all the way human inside a system built on dehumanization excited us and motivated us to try to be smarter and more engaged teachers.

Each of our students was serving a term of life without possibility of parole, or what they called "death by incarceration." It's fair to say that had any of them had a $100,000 legal defense, the sentence might have been severe, but it would not have been a sentence to die in prison. Each came to prison, as most do, with a satchel full of what the judicial system euphemistically calls "mitigating circumstances": untreated health and mental health issues, poverty, homelessness, failing schools, abuse. These don't count for much in courtrooms where lived-life with all of its messiness and complexity is overwhelmed by two rigid and static narratives in fateful competition with one another: guilt or innocence. We knew something about our students from those narrow narratives written decades ago—those stories were serious, often true, but always incomplete. We also knew them as people who had worked steadily for several years toward rehabilitation and toward making positive contributions to their communities, intrepidly pursuing educational and professional certificates that attested to their hard work and determination—and those, too, are incomplete. Neither narrative fully captures the men we saw showing up in class each week.

Our friend Renaldo Hudson, who spent thirty-eight years in Illinois prisons, twelve on death row, often says, in effect: "I like the 'second chances' programs, but you should know that I, and most of the people I was inside with, never had a *first* chance." Mitigating factors. He also notes: "I like the Innocence Project, too, and there's certainly a lot of work to do to exonerate and free the wrongfully convicted. But I was guilty of the crime I was sentenced for, and I'm still a human being—after thirty-eight years, what more?" It's not a matter of condoning or excusing but, rather, of recognizing and respecting growth and change, and at a certain point a question of grace and mercy.

Renaldo Hudson brings to mind another small piece from *The Brothers Karamazov*, a sermon by the elderly Father Zosima in which he insists on the social dimension of guilt, and the need for both responsibility and forgiveness: "You should know, my dear ones, that every individual is undoubtedly responsible for everyone and everything on earth, not only with respect to general guilt, but also each individual is responsible for every single person and all human beings on earth."[18] So, Renaldo should not have stood trial alone; next to him in the dock should have been a school and a legal system that failed him, a society that marginalized him, an economic system that injured him. In other words, all of us.

7

CREATING CRAWL SPACES
FOR FREEDOM

I want to be remembered as a person
who wanted to be free...
so other people also
would be free.

—ROSA PARKS

Sometimes we ask, what can one person do to bring about the kinds of changes that would lean toward justice and joy, peace and freedom, balance and fairness? The first necessary step is to stop being *one person*. Walk away from "me," and move toward "we." Make a list of ten concrete steps you could take in the next five weeks to move from "me" toward "we."

— REFLECTION SEVEN: ORGANIZING FREEDOM —

One of Karl Marx's most famous dictums is carved onto his gravestone: "The philosophers have only *interpreted* the world, in various ways. The point, however, is to *change* it."[1]

Exactly—so beautifully put, and so true.

Yes, the first step is opening our eyes, seeing the world as fully as we're able, taking it all in, studying and researching, seeking and telling the truth, searching for more, unraveling all that we see, and then opening our eyes again. Making meaning, making sense, *interpreting* and constructing a world.

Another step is allowing ourselves to feel the world throbbing inside of us, to hear its rhythmic heartbeat in synch with our own—to be astonished at all the beauty and the splendor and the magnificence we see in all directions, and by all the unnecessary suffering and undeserved pain human beings visit upon one another. And then, of course, rising up and acting in response to what the known demands of us—to *do something*, as Nina Simone instructed earlier. Interpreting the world isn't enough; we must try to change it. This takes us into the realm of strategy and tactics, where we state our aims and objectives—and, most important, our *values*—as clearly as we can, make and implement a plan, and organize ourselves for action.

But before we go further, let's remember a basic fact about revolutionary change—or, more modestly, about even baby steps toward social justice: change is never accomplished by an individual acting alone, no matter how brilliant, well intentioned, hard working, or virtuous. There is simply no example of justice achieved without a large number of people in motion and in cahoots, variously referred to by the powerful and the protectors of the status quo as "the mob," "the rabble," "the horde," or "the riffraff," and known (by those of us who consider the status quo a state of general emergency) as the public, the masses, the extraordinary ordinary people.

Neither is there a single case of justice secured without action—and that always involves a measure of discomfort and some amount of risk. It takes a lot to change the world: anger and impatience, generosity and love, study and reflection, learning and teaching, organizing and activism, strategy and tactics. And courage.

A uthentic courage is at its heart moral reflection or moral instinct leading to ethical action. One could display a kind of fearlessness or daring or disregard for the obvious physical risks in certain situations, but if those acts of "bravery" are based on delusion or derangement or ignorance, they're just foolishness. Or if the apparent bravery and risk on display is deployed for selfish or antisocial purposes ("He boldly crashed through the barrier, risked life and limb to crack the Coop's safe, and then made his escape, skateboarding over the rickety bridge with the worker 'collective savings balanced on his forehead"), it cannot be celebrated, or judged an act of moral courage. Moral courage is a central virtue in a free society and essential to the project of advancing democracy. If you consider democracy a verb, and not just a noun, then its oxygen is supplied by people willing to stand up for justice, peace, enlightenment, and liberation, and thereby recalibrating the meaning of freedom.

Moral courage is a layered and complex idea, but, in broad strokes, it's relatively easy to describe: different people in vastly different circumstances, deploying a broad range of tactics and strategies have stood up for more peace, more equality, more recognition, more transparency, more participatory arrangements, and more collective freedom. Courage.

But most of us most of the time act as others act in our community—we behave in the acceptable and prevailing manner. In a society marked by slavery or concentration camps or war or racism or predatory and exploitative relations to production, acting conventionally means doing harm. It takes a developing moral imagination, and the summoning of real moral courage, to stand against that. And standing up is the lifeblood of freedom.

The idea that moral courage is picking the box marked "good" and rejecting the box marked "bad" in a clean and decontextualized social field of obvious alternatives is a myth. Those happy labels could as easily be called "conventional" and "unconventional" because most of us act conventionally and assume that we are, in fact, "good" people. In real life, moral choices never come in those neat packages. If they did, moral reasoning would be straightforward and simple (and would not require *reasoning* at all—the compass would be preset and operating continuously on automatic pilot), but, because they don't, we're confronted at every turn with complex dilemmas and messy choices. And authentic choices are typically characterized by loss as well as gain.

Mamie Till-Mobley's insistence, in the midst of shattering grief, that her son Emmett's mutilated body appear in an open casket in order to show the world the face of white supremacy in 1955 was courage on bright display. It was an act that made us all a little freer. So were Colin Kaepernick's decision to take a knee in 2016, refusing to stand for the ritual playing of the national anthem before NFL games, as a protest against police brutality and social injustice; Muhammed Ali's refusal in 1967 to serve in the US military, expressing solidarity with the Vietnamese people; the Reverend Martin Luther King Jr.'s speech of April 4, 1967, "Beyond Vietnam," when he broke with many of his most powerful allies by linking racial justice to global and economic justice, peace, and socialism; Fred Korematsu's arrest in 1942 for refusing internment, the overturning of his arrest in 1983, and being honored with the Presidential Medal of Freedom in 1998; the Fort Hood Three refusing to be sent to "quell civil unrest" in Chicago in 1968; Bree Newsome Bass scaling the flag pole at the South Carolina state capitol in 2015 and removing the Confederate flag—these are all examples of freedom's call and response. I could go on for pages and pages: the Tank Man in 1989; Mandela's speech at Rivonia; Ida B. Wells's investigative reporting; Shirley Chisholm's run for president; Fidel and comrades in the *Granma*; the antiwar monks of Vietnam; Bobby Sands's fast in a British prison; Martin Sostre's refusal of all work assignments in a New York prison as a protest against mistreatment; the Flint sit-down strike in the 1930s; Ethel Rosenberg's unwillingness to save her own life by testifying against her husband; Seymour Hirsch breaking the My Lai story (and the soldiers who blew the whistle by speaking to him); Kujo Lewis's request for reparations in 1865; Chelsea Manning, Julian Assange, and Edward Snowden releasing classified documents; Albert Woodfox, in solitary confinement in Angola prison for decades, exposing and denouncing the carceral state and the Prison Nation; Yuri Kochiyama standing with Malcolm X; the undocumented and unafraid movement in Chicago and the work of the Immigrant Youth Justice League in 2009 leading to the "Come out of the Shadows" campaign in 2010; the Attica Brothers in New York in the 1970s, and the Death Row Ten in Illinois in the 1990s; the 1969 occupation of Alcatraz Island by Native Americans—all of these acts of courage are also attempts to perform freedom in practice.

Action is risky in tiny and monumental ways: you may offend a friend, you may be thought ill of, and on a different register, you may be arrested, beaten, or even killed. When someone manifests courage, there are no guarantees whatsoever. And while it's impossible to know in advance, the power of moral courage is potentially infinite. The day before Rosa Parks refused to move to the back of the bus, the Civil Rights Movement seemed impossible; the day after, it was called inevitable.

If we open our eyes, we will see moral courage everywhere: in the streets and the neighborhoods, in schools and workplaces, in houses of worship, in arts and cultural organizations. I see young, brave organizers of groups like Black Lives Matter!; the Let Us Breathe Collective; Good Kids, Mad City; Assata's Daughters; and AirGo framing the debates in hopeful, radically imaginative ways. Moral courage is predictably lacking in the halls of Congress (OK—the Squad is a small exception shining a ray of light into the thick and heavy darkness), the political class, the Pentagon, Wall Street. But look to the young; courage comes more naturally to them. When you consider it for a moment, it makes sense that the average age of a runaway slave in the 1850s was sixteen.

Courage and action are parts of the freedom struggle, and so are comrades and allies, supporters and friends. So is thinking and planning, strategy and tactics developing a long-range plan toward transformation, and taking the baby steps and the giant leaps to get there.

Strategy asks us to *name the moment*—that is, to analyze our situation as clearly as we can on political/historical/cultural grounds, to illuminate the unfreedoms we are hoping to abolish, and to make a concrete analysis of concrete conditions. It's impossible to struggle effectively unless you work toward knowing both where you are and where you want to go. Naming the moment, identifying your forces and allies as well as the powers aligned in opposition, looking squarely at the contradictions—that's how we think strategically.

We're in the mix and on the move. We might sometimes feel a bit like the bewildered Alice stuck at the crossroads in Wonderland, famously asking directions of the Cheshire Cat: "Would you tell me, please, which way I ought to go from here?" "That depends a good deal on where you want to get to," said the Cat. "I don't much care where—" said Alice. "Then it doesn't matter which way you go," said the Cat. "—so long as I get *somewhere*," Alice added as explanation. "Oh, you're sure to do that," said the Cat, "if you only walk long enough."[2]

Unlike Alice, we care deeply about where we're going—we are the midwives of a kaleidoscope of possible futures, and it matters a lot. We're sure to get somewhere, of course, but the *where* is critical to us. Will it be a place of more joy and more love, or less? Will it be a society of peace and greater participatory democracy, of more robust justice and an expanded sense of freedom? Will it be a place fit for all of our children?

Note, however, how easy it can be to arrive at a complex and well-developed sense of the moment and its demands, to state purposes, and then to fail to revisit, rethink, revise, or refine—remember that a moment is a moment is a moment, and it's only a moment. Things today are a bit different from yesterday, and things will certainly be different tomorrow. History is on the move, the world is churning and turning, the situation evolving—everything must change. We can't name the moment once and for all; rather, we can, each and all of us, develop the habit and the practice of waking up on each new morning, and naming the moment over and over, again and again.

Tactics, the wildly diverse forms we develop to advance the strategy, can be large or small, short term or long term. Say our goal is to end mass incarceration, and we recognize that there is work to do to change the narrative about crime and the criminal legal system, as well as about who the human beings are who are forced to live in cages now. We will need to humanize those who have been systematically dehumanized, and we will need to challenge the myths that link public safety to caging. Our tactics might include campaigning to end cash bail, mobilizing opposition in a community where the state proposes building a new prison, organizing an advocacy group with families impacted by the system, publishing the art and poetry and essays of incarcerated human beings in order to counteract the prevailing "monsterfication" and "worst of the worst" stereotypes, developing alternative jobs/careers for working-class people recruited to serve as guards and clerks in the punishment bureaucracies, disrupting the school-to-prison pipeline (or, as my comrade Dave Stovall calls it, "the school-to-prison nexus," indicating a more entangled and intentional connection), educating the public about the link between poverty and prisons and the obvious failures of the current system, planning a series of direct actions starting with sitting in at the governor's office demanding mass commutations for certain categories of crimes, creating a broad coalition that can draw a range of organizations into a united front, proposing laws and abolitionist policies and then lobbying legislators, electing progressive criminal legal officials like state's attorneys, and teaching journalists about racial and economic bias in crime reporting. And more.

Generating a vision, long-range planning, motivating, goal-setting, enlarging and nurturing our hope quotient, engaging in the nitty-gritty and the nuts and bolts—all of this is part of the work of an organizer. I've been an activist and an agitator, an agnostic/skeptic/dissident, a rebel and a revolutionary my entire adult life. I've also always been an organizer or a teacher, and I realized early on that being an effective organizer and being a good teacher, looked at from a certain angle of regard, are pretty much indistinguishable—teaching and organizing often feel to me like the same thing.

A teacher is constantly thinking ahead, looking way down the road to where they want to go, planning and setting goals, and diving into the dailiness that defines the work. It's in the day-to-day spadework that the lofty goals and the best-laid plans are accomplished or go off the tracks. Any collection of real people (as opposed to cardboard cutouts represented in lesson plans or union campaigns) is dynamic, complex, jittery, squirrelly, and on the move. Human beings defy on some level being "managed" at all, and seasoned teachers know that classrooms are where lesson plans come to life in surprising ways—or go to die.

Like teachers, effective organizers become accustomed to perpetual uncertainty, contingency, and experimentation; we nourish, then, a tolerance for confusion, flux, and vulnerability, and learn skills of dialogue and improvisation (unrehearsed, and, therefore, always unpredictable and a little risky) as we build toward spontaneous cooperation and constant learning. We work hard for a goal, and we stop to doubt, to question, to retool, and to begin again. The most agile people I've known are labor and community organizers—and teachers.

When a community organizer knocks on a door, they assume an intelligence in the people they face—we know that there's deep potential and real capacity in the person at the doorstep. We're not there as do-gooders; we're there to respect and protect and unite with the agency and power of the people. We're there to learn as well as to teach, to listen as well as to speak, to link arms and walk together—solidarity, not service—on the long and winding road toward transformation and freedom.

And transformation is key. Organizers (and teachers) are in their hearts agents of change. We want to change the consciousness of our students, our neighbors, and our fellow workers; we want to change our own consciousness at the same time. And, again, we want to change the world in the direction of more justice and more peace, more joy and more love, more of the good life shared all round.

One of the most difficult aspects of organizing is the recognition that you must *let learn*—that's right, the organizer creates an environment for learning, gathers resources, introduces contradictions, and sets in motion the conditions for discovery and surprise, for themselves as well as others, and then . . . let's go. Learning is the work of the people themselves. The organizer or teacher has to *let learn*, and that means sometimes being quiet, taking a backseat, encouraging others to take center stage. The goal is empowerment, enhanced agency, enlightenment, and liberation, but an authentic education is never *given* to passive people or empty vessels waiting quietly in rows. Rather, empowerment and genuine learning, in order to be sturdy and reliable, is *seized* by them—the energy released at those moments is palpable, and the result is transformation in every direction.

Because we live day by day, immersed in what is—the world as such—imagining a landscape much different from what's immediately before us requires a combination of somethings: seeds, surely, desire, yes, effort, of course, always effort, idealism and romance, maybe, necessity and desperation at times, and a vision of dazzling possibility at other times. Every desire does not flow inevitably toward freedom, but freedom makes an appearance when desire is made legible and then engaged. We need a sense of urgency and a sense of balance. We need serious thinking and planning and experimenting. Occasionally what's required is the willful enthusiasm to dance out on a limb—the practice of freedom. We all do better when we're holding hands with others out on that limb. Organize!

. . . ABOLITION IS THE ANSWER

**"POEM NUMBER TWO ON BELL'S THEOREM,
OR THE NEW PHYSICALITY OF LONG DISTANCE LOVE"**
*There is no chance that we will fall apart
There is no chance
There are no parts.*

—JUNE JORDAN

Take a minute to reflect on these questions, and jot down your first responses: Where are we on the clock of the universe? What does the known demand of us, here and now? What is the urgency? What is to be done? And where do we go from here—chaos or community, slavery or freedom?

— REFLECTION EIGHT: FREEDOM AND ABOLITION —

Our kids were born abolitionists—they had no choice in the matter. Like all children, ours were thrust into a going-world, a world not of their own making nor of their choosing, but a world that was theirs nonetheless. The world they were born into was already up and running, and their job, like every other child who ever lived or ever will live, was to learn to walk, at first catching up with the forward-charging world, then running alongside, and soon enough sprinting ahead, passing their elders at breakneck speed, branching out onto curious and novel side roads, forging their own unique pathways, fleeing, perhaps, or spinning around in direct opposition. That's life itself, the answer to a universal question: What will I make of what I've been made?

Their parents—us—weren't their choice, just the first random toss of the cosmic dice, with a zillion chance happenings still to come. No one chooses their parents, of course, nor their brief moment in the sun. Everyone lands somewhere specific with a context and a ready-made set of circumstances: this country or that community, these fortunes or misfortunes, those accidental advantages or disadvantages. But for better or worse, our kids got the Upper West Side of New York, and they got us, and as part of the package they inherited an extended family of rebels and revolutionaries, freedom fighters, race-traitors, and abolitionists—they were dancing the dialectic with their very first steps.

My friend Maya Schenwar told me recently that she'd read her four-year-old a children's book about Native grandmothers organizing a struggle to stop an oil pipeline from being built on tribal land. The pipeline would destroy valuable wildlife habitat, spoil farmland, endanger water sources, and add to the crisis of global warming and environmental collapse. What stood out for the child was the wisdom and courage of the old women—they studied and educated themselves and their neighbors, they got the community to stand up together, they stood tall, and they stopped construction—and so the child wanted to make a sign and join the grandmothers' demonstration. "And what would your sign say?" Maya asked. The response was quick and sharp: "No Pipeline!"

A four-year-old doesn't need to consider alternate routes that would endanger different rivers, or financial compensation for ruined land, or the relative value of an endangered owl and cheaper gas from tar sands. No. The moral position was crystal clear and unencumbered: no pipeline! A natural abolitionist.

Children spring to the ethical heart of abolition like fish cavorting in the water—it's their natural habitat, and they get it. Kids are intuitive abolitionists because abolition points to solid solutions, and young people live in a world of concrete operations.

If you wonder about books for young children on complex and controversial topics, that genie has been out of the bottle for decades. There are wonderful, thoughtful, compassionate books for young children (and older children, and young adults and older adults) on women's equality, racism, peace, environmental justice, gender rights, disability, war, empire, mental health . . . on practically everything. There are biographies that inspire empathy, celebrate accomplishment and resilience across world cultures. The issue goes beyond scope and variety, however, and urges equitable and uncensored access, and trusting children to pursue their own interests and engage with their own curiosities. Activists like Daphne Muse in Berkeley, California, and Judi Minter and BJ Richards in Chicago have assembled thousands of anti-racist, anti-sexist, inclusive, and delightful books for kids of all ages, and they share the wonder, offering advice and counsel for parents and teachers.

Well, there aren't books on literally everything, of course—there's still more to know, more to learn, more to see and experience. As James Baldwin once said, "American history is longer, larger, more various, more beautiful, and more terrible than anything anyone has ever said about it."[1] So, if you can think of an urgent issue that's not been written about for kids, reach for your pencils and paper, and get busy!

And if you worry about the above example being *propaganda*, note that the advertising industry wraps its rapacious claws tightly around our children's minds while singing siren songs on a continuous loop into their innocent ears, and that Florida has outlawed the teaching of history except as a set of fictional myths ginned up by a small clique of politicians, and, to take only one egregious example out of zillions, that the American Coal Foundation, the coal industry's lobbying arm, lavishly funds "educational materials" like a colorful classroom map called "The United States of Energy" that Friends of the Earth labeled "corporate brainwashing."[2]

"That's not fair!"—the mantra of most three-year-olds—echoed through our fifth-floor walkup for years, and it carried the same indignant tone in our family, whether referring to the smallest injustice on the playground or to some monstrous police murder on the streets of Brooklyn. Nuclear bombs were not fair, and when we joined one million others in Central Park wearing No Nukes T-shirts, our kids saw people who didn't just pay attention to the evils of the world but were also willing to resist and to try to abolish those evils. There were no T-shirts advocating "Some Nukes" or "Only Tactical Nukes, Please." Nope, "No Nukes" was the whole deal—abolition!

A character in Danielle Evans's novella *The Office of Historical Corrections* says, "The beauty of motherhood is that all the choices are wrong." Asked by her friend if it's terrifying being a parent, she responds, "Yes . . . It's like every day since Octavia was born I've had to choose between trying to do the best I can for her and trying to do the best I can for the world she has to live in."[3] Dancing another dialectic.

Our oldest said he knew nukes were bad and also gigantic—"as big as tall buildings"—and he wondered how freakishly big the war-makers' airplanes must be to carry such monstrosities. As big as the Empire State Building? Concrete operational questions—honest answers. And, always, fairness mattered and activism counted. But abolition ruled.

We had reinvented ourselves years earlier as activists in the peace and justice struggles of mid-century America: We strived to be comrades with the Black Freedom Movement, community organizers in poor areas of the city, militants and troublemakers opposed to US militarism and empire. We built communes and collectives in order to live out our utopian visions of what could be or should be but was not yet, seeds of a possible world planted in the dirt of the dying one—the world as such, and the only world we knew. Everything old was questioned, criticized, and put on trial; everything new and unknown was worth a try . . . or two or three.

We vowed to become new women and new men in order to be worthy of the world of our dreams—so we smashed monogamy and experimented with "free love," grew our own food in vacant lots, gathered up garbage during a city workers' strike to deposit at the gates of high culture, made tofu from scratch, gave out free food in the parks,

knocked on doors regularly, fought the cops in the streets when necessary, endorsed unruly flesh and anarchist activity, and dove head
first into the great simultaneous circus show of youth culture. Did it
"work"? Not exactly, but we were enacting that age-old rhythm mentioned earlier: try, fail, try again, fail again—fail better. We always act
without guarantees and in situations not of our choosing, and we can
never know for sure what the consequences of our actions will be. And
still we must act, and in the aftermath, we can judge our efforts with
a straightforward pedagogical standard: Did we learn? Did we teach?
Then we move on to try again.

When our kids were born, they joined our tribe, of course, and expanded and enriched our wayward culture in miraculous ways. They
altered our daily routines and rhythms dramatically, but our anarchist/
socialist political dispositions and our experimental impulses remained.
The mode and manner of our new family was shot through with politics
and activism—the kids were born onto picket lines, our lively apart-
ment abuzz with friends and comrades, potluck dinners, organizing
projects and action planning sessions, meetings and discussions, along
with the ordinary management of everyday life: overnights, play dates,
laundry, groceries, and paying the damn rent. Because we never owned
a TV, conversation was the liveliest current in the room and our kids'
earliest words and phrases included "Peace now" and "No racism." Even
without a literal understanding of every detail of every cause, there was
a kind of child-friendly and joyful resistance on offer, a sense that we
always stood up somehow for peace and freedom—against racism and
for fairness. Once, leaving an Aqua Tots swimming class at the Y, we
were swept into a feminist march to Times Square, happily chanting
along: "Our bodies, ourselves!" and "No more porn!" We cruised off
to get pizza, and once we settled into our booth, one of the kids said,
"That was great. Why don't we want any more corn?" Today I imagine
we would carry signs demanding the decriminalization of sex work and
the right to organize a union.

Malcolm X famously noted that Black people seemed forever to have an abundance of Washingtons and Jeffersons and Lincolns in their family trees, but white people didn't even have a twig or a leaf for Nat Turner or Frederick Douglass or Harriett Tubman. Why, he asked rhetorically and pointedly, why the color line—even when it comes to naming the babies? We chose to take Malcolm's observation as a practical matter, and so we named our firstborn Zayd Osceola, to remember a Black Panther brother killed by the police in New Jersey, and at the same time to raise up a Seminole leader who never surrendered to the US policy of relocation and extermination; we called our second Malik Cochise, this time in honor of Malcolm himself as well as a renowned First Nations legend, the great Apache guerrilla fighter.

Chesa—formally Chesa Jackson Gilbert Boudin—bounded into our family and crash-landed in our lives when he was fourteen months old and his birth parents, Kathy Boudin and David Gilbert, working with the Black Liberation Army, were arrested in Nyack, New York, for the attempted armed robbery of a Brinks armored truck in which a guard and two police were killed. His name was already attached, and it fit right in: Chesa, a Swahili word for dancing feet, and Jackson, taken from Soledad Brother George Jackson, murdered by prison guards at San Quentin. His prized T-shirt was a silk-screen portrait of Rosa Parks in dignified refusal.

We had two kids, and we were living in Manhattan; Kathy and David had fourteen-month-old Chesa, living with her parents in Greenwich Village since the catastrophe at Nyack. We'd known and loved Kathy and David forever, and they were family—our brother and our sister—and, whatever else, family should take care of one another, especially in times of crisis. The pulse and measure of our lives was fully tuned to the complex rhythms of raising young kids, and here we were, fully immersed in the joyful cacophony of a toddler orchestra. Yes, there would be room for one more. And if, God forbid, anything catastrophic were ever to overwhelm us, who, of all the people in the world, would we want to step up for our beloveds? We would want us, of course.

When we first visited David and Kathy in prison, they were fearful for Chesa, hungry for news, and worried about next steps. We broached the idea of taking him into our family, and they leapt as if at the last lifeboat pulling swiftly away from a sinking ship. "Yes, yes, we will coparent for a time, and when we get out . . . " Reality was still some ways away. Soon Bernardine was locked up in federal prison for refusing to testify before a federal grand jury investigating the Brinks robbery—civil contempt. Visiting prisons became a regular part of our family routine.

Kathy and David and Bernardine were all learning together how to be present to their kids in these terrible circumstances, practical ways to parent from a distance—applicable to hospitalization or divorce or death, forced migration and military deployment, but, in our cases, applied to the separation of prison. They each wrote long, intricate chapter books for the kids, and solicited advice and counsel from them on the phone about the direction of the next week's installment. Bernardine created a growing catalogue of riddles and jokes for every visit, and she made a crossword puzzle every week for Zayd based on themes of his choice: favorite foods or best fruit, Central Park and dogs, baseball and mommies coming home. We were honest about what had happened but always following the kids' leads on how far to go and what territory to enter.

One year we marked Passover with a seder at the women's prison. The theme of freedom from bondage is universal at Passover, and our rewritten Haggadah focused on US imperialism, Palestinian freedom, and political prisoners—it was an abolitionist Haggadah. At the end of the traditional "feast" the rabbi hid the afikomen. After much search-ing in the visiting room, the kids found it, and when the rabbi said they had one wish, Malik said, "I wish all the women here could go home today." Eventually they did all come home: Bernardine after less than a year in lockup—and never testifying—Kathy after twenty-two years, and David after forty years and ten days.

In those early years we were part of a homemade communal child-care community on the Upper West Side of Manhattan called BJ's Kids. Fairness was a central value at BJ's, and the deeply radical and profoundly ethical slogan of the Wobblies from a hundred years earlier was a poster on the wall: "An injury to one is an injury to all!" That standard was easily grasped by preschoolers.

We tried to speak an anti-oppressive language at BJ's—"firefighter," not "fireman"—and our block area fought racism and sexism: the figures included a Black woman doctor, a Latina firefighter, a male nurse. Reality imposed itself, however, and it was clear that the firehouse across the street was staffed by all white firemen. On a field trip Caitlin, one of the four-year-olds, asked the fireman showing us around when we would get a woman firefighter in the station, and our guide exploded in derisive laughter: "A woman! We don't want any women! The neighborhood would burn down!" That's not fair, Caitlin said, and back at BJ's she dictated letters to the mayor and the newspapers.

We built solidarity between kids and adults, and with everyone in reach. Solidarity, not service, and not hierarchy. There was an open promise of acceptance, care, and repair at BJ's Kids. No one was a target of instruction; everyone was a dynamic and growing part of the whole. We dove freely into the wide, wild world, and swam as hard as we could toward a distant horizon, powered by experimentation, discovery, and surprise, always asking the next question and the next, and then the next.

BJ's Kids was raising abolitionists, people who would stand up against subjugation, people who together constructed a shared space of fairness and kindness, folks who were a prelude to the possible, and willing to ask the big question: What kind of world do we need to build in order to live free?

What would it mean to abolish private insurance, advertising, private drug companies, landlords, private homes? What about abolishing private profit and wage slavery? What worlds could we build then? Or, what would it mean to abolish the family? Heresy! But is it? "The family" plays a role analogous to the "American dream" in our dominant culture—anything at all can be inscribed on the words for any political purpose. Let's abolish both.

"The family," it's worth noting, is the site of more sexual and physical abuse, assault, and murder than any other institution, more than the church and the schools and the workplace together. It's a site of unpaid labor and hidden exploitation. "Dysfunctional family" is a redundant term—they're all dysfunctional, all outposts of racial capitalism, asked to shoulder unbearable burdens that should be the responsibility of the larger community. Abolishing male supremacy, patriarchy, gender hierarchies, and forced dependence is the right thing to do, and each is embodied in concentrated and congealed form in the romanticized family.

Abolishing the family would not mean abolishing commitment or love, and in fact abolition may liberate love, release new energy, and represent a deeper expression of care and affection. Love means nothing if it doesn't mean love for specific human beings. That special love can be generalized, performing as a model for treating everyone as worthy, but it does not work the other way around: saints and orthodox liturgists and dogmatic ideologues claim to love humanity or "the people" in general—a claim that allows them to squash particular individuals, often in large numbers, in pursuit of whatever Grand Plan is on offer.

The "American dream" and the "American family" are the domestic twins of American exceptionalism and perform as a kind of social Rorschach test. The dream could mean a one-family home in the suburbs with a two-car garage to some, marital bliss plus two beautiful and above-average children to others, or a partridge in a pear tree. Maybe it's job security or a career, good health or a pension when you're old, a college education for the kids, or season tickets to the Cubs. Yes, yes, yes—achieving the American dream includes picking up some or, preferably, all of the above.

But the dream includes rampant consumerism and unchecked acquisition, the freedom to acquire unlimited cash and shop till you drop, the embrace of a culture of malignant individualism. And individualism is a core capitalist value. In Aaron Sorkin's TV show *Newsroom*, a hard-bitten reporter decides to cut the crap when a college student asks, "Why is America the greatest country in the world?" He points out that the United States is 7th in the world in literacy, 49th in life expectancy, and 178th in infant mortality. "We lead the world in only three categories," he asserts: number of incarcerated fellow citizens, military spending, and number of adults who believe in angels. He could now add that in international surveys, the US ranks first in "individualistic." The powerful reject the social, the communal, or the collective, as the country wallows in goblin mode.

The logic of prison abolition was first explained to me by the great freedom fighter Angela Davis: Prison is not just a place, she said, it's an ideology. The ideology limits our imaginations and shuts down our capacity to think more broadly and more bravely. We need to wonder what might lie beyond prison, beyond making a better or more functional prison system—the focus of too many reform conversations—and initiate massive conversations about decarceration, that is, bringing folks home and shutting prisons down. We have to think of ways to close the front door, the pipeline feeding the beast as more and more people are funneled in, and open wide the back door.

Mass incarceration—the caging and control of criminalized populations and marginalized people deemed disposable—is a major part of the afterlife of slavery, and prison abolition is the next step in that long historic project of abolition and Black freedom. And, as we imagine dramatic change, we should also anticipate future attempts to contain and control, for just as Jim Crow followed abolition, and mass incarceration followed Jim Crow, some evil expression of white supremacy and Black containment yet unseen lurks just around the corner.

Over time Mariame Kaba taught me, as did Ruth Wilson Gilmore and Erica Meiners, Alice Kim and Beth Richie, Renaldo Hudson and Albert Woodfox. We talked about abolitionist values: liberation, community restoration, and shared fate as opposed to the hardening practices of cruelty and punishment, revenge and retribution. We were reminded of the ten renowned words uttered by Justice Harry Blackmun in 1994 when he announced publicly that he had become a death penalty abolitionist: "I no longer shall tinker with the machinery of death."⁴ Blackmun wasn't searching for ways to make state-sanctioned murder more efficient or more palatable; he wanted to get out of the death business altogether. Let's get out of the caging business altogether, we said. Let's not tinker with the machinery of mass incarceration.

The "prison nation" is an intolerable abomination. Once you see it, you can't unsee it, and joining the insurgency becomes an urgent necessity. Modern misdemeanor law can be traced directly to the Black Codes after slavery that criminalized ordinary actions (loitering, staying out late at night) precisely to control formerly enslaved people.⁵ The explosive growth of the prison population followed close on the heels of the powerful modern Black Freedom Movement, criminalizing whole communities and exacting collective punishment.

I proposed prison abolition publicly—and a little anxiously—in a talk I gave about Freedom Schools at the University of Pittsburgh. Most of my talk was well received, even when I pointed out, as I always do, that the existence of an American gulag stretching the length and breadth of the country meant that you were never far from a prison, but there was a general sense of disbelief when I said I thought prisons should be abolished. The first question from the floor was a request to clarify the point, which I did, saying I thought we should work toward closing all the prisons since they were institutions of capricious cruelty and congealed violence. The next student up worried that I was kidding, and I assured them I was not, and followed up by politely accusing me of utopian romanticism and unrealistic idealism. Guilty, I said, of the idealism, but not of being unrealistic. The next person who spoke tried to show me the error of my logic and painted a terrifying picture of a world ruled by mass murderers (*Hmm*, I thought), pointing specifically to John Wayne Gacy, the gruesome serial killer who was electrocuted soon after Illinois reinstated the death penalty, a person about whom my interrogator had seemingly encyclopedic knowledge. I'm convinced, I said after an exhaustive portrayal, I give up! Okay, that's one cell, I said, so who else? I'll give you Henry Kissinger and Dick Cheney, so now we have three prison cells total—a far cry from the millions we support in reality.

This led to a discussion I've had countless times, and it begins with an exercise in the form of a question: Can we—right now—generate a thousand alternatives to caging people? It turns out we can, so let's

- Build "Community Restorative Justice" projects—spaces where perpetrators and victims can meet with peers and neighbors, community organizers and social workers, to discuss how to repair the harm inflicted by misbehavior
- Redirect all misdemeanor offenses away from criminal court with its attendant culture of cruelty, humiliation, and punishment toward counseling, rehab, or anger management for some, and technological support (a simple breathalyzer device, for example, attached to a vehicle before it can be driven) for others
- Do away with "truth-in-sentencing," mandatory minimum sentences, "three strikes you're out," sentence enhancements, money bail, and other punitive measures that serve to swell the prison population
- Restore or create opportunities to reduce time inside with policies like day-for-day good time practices
- Immediately release all aging people in prison—say, anyone over sixty, who has done twenty years or more in prison—and grant mass commutation to entire categories of imprisoned people: women resisting violence, people possessing drugs, folks convicted on the testimony of dirty cops, people convicted of crimes when they were minors and have served significant sentences, and more
- Develop a prisoner's cooperative to operate the institutions, making decisions collectively about all matters concerning food, health care, education, and social services, the organization of work and leisure, and relations with outside institutions including religious, educational, and business organizations

That wasn't hard at all, and we only have 994 to go.

Some of this may sound a bit like fiddling with the machinery of caging, but let's not be dogmatic hard-liners when actual people could breathe more freely with just a bit of tinkering. The goal is not to *reform* or compromise enslavement, subjugation, abuse, cruelty, persecution, avariciousness, exploitation, predation, and oppression, so, OK, tinker, but let's never lose sight of the north star: an end to prisons—abolition.

Similarly, talk of "defunding the police" is ridiculed in the commercial press, but we should ask ourselves, what qualities would make policing in a free and democratic society different from policing in an unfree or authoritarian society? Or, what is the link between aggressive and expensive policing and public safety? Is there any evidence that caging people makes us safer? And then we can perform once more the exercise we did regarding prison abolition, brainstorming one thousand steps toward police abolition:

- Get guns off the streets, including guns in the hands of state agents.
- Create massive public works programs.
- Build homes for the unhoused.
- Bring the endowments of all private schools, colleges, and universities under public and democratic control, and organize the redistribution of those resources toward a system of free quality education for all.
- Use a public-health frame to rethink issues of violence.
- Grant guaranteed income supports to the unemployed.
- Provide a guaranteed living-wage stipend, free housing, and good childcare to anyone living at or below the poverty line and attending high school or community college.
- Create a system of single-payer, universal health care.
- Generously create and support community mental health programs.
- Decriminalize illegal drugs and expand drug treatment centers to meet the real needs of people caught in the grip of addiction.

wow!!! Only 990 more items to discover and fight for!

I'm helping to organize a national network called CopagandaWatch, a collection of people dedicated to abolishing propaganda concerning public safety and policing, and replacing it with accurate data, verifiable facts, and compelling analysis. The term is the invention of the activist attorney Alec Karakatsanis. Here's my "dictionary definition":

"Copaganda (n.) Biased or misleading information generated to promote and publicize the point-of-view of organized police forces; deliberate misinformation spread by law enforcement bureaucracies and their political and media allies to confuse or pacify citizens; a coordinated effort to indoctrinate the public by creating a powerful positive narrative around police work and policing that is immune from fact-checking, counter-narratives, or lived experiences, and takes on, then, the odor of common sense; the Hollywood/TV spin on crime (the good-guys in blue versus the bad-guys in black) that dominates the nightly news; cop propaganda."

Examples of the word used in a sentence:

The mayor's description of the fatal police shooting was once again an instance of official copaganda, *relying entirely on statements from the police department's office of public relations.*

The "exclusive" re-creation of the crime scene on Channel 2 Live Action News was copaganda *based solely on lengthy interviews with two supervising detectives.*

The profile of Officer Friendly in the "Features" section of Sunday's paper was a classic puff piece—incurious, uncritical, one-sided—and another in a long and familiar line of copaganda *stories that dominate the local press.*

Copaganda foregrounds petty crime and presents it in all its gaudy detail while downplaying, hiding, or entirely ignoring other more serious crimes. Crime rates tend to capture a small subset of police-reported crimes committed by the poor and to exclude crimes committed by the wealthy. For example, property crime data reported by the police excludes most property crime, including wage theft by employers (which costs low-wage workers about *$50 billion per year*, three times more than all *police-reported property crime* that makes its way into "crime rates" and the nightly news), and tax evasion (which steals about *$1 trillion* every year, twenty times more than all wage theft and sixty-three times more than all police-reported property crime combined).[6] The vast majority of all other types of crime—such as air and water pollution crimes, police perjury, prosecutor obstruction of justice, government corruption, insider stock trading, foreign bribery—are never reported to police and rarely pursued by prosecutors, and therefore they never show up in police-reported crime rates. Further, police-reported *crime rates are generally lower* in societies that spend less money on police, prosecutors, and prisons and that spend more money on health care, treatment, early childhood education, youth activities, poverty reduction, and wellness.[7]

CopagandaWatch is skeptical of a legal system that demands a high standard of evidence—beyond a reasonable doubt—to convict a person of a crime but allows caging millions without a shred of evidence that it does any good. We resist faith-based, fact-free approaches to questions of justice and safety. We're critical of politicians who crow about public safety unless safety would require less inequality. We seek fact-based information.

CopagandaWatch engages people from a wide range of backgrounds, ages, regions, political perspectives, and occupations, including students and teachers, academics and scholars, professionals and laborers, fact-checkers and citizen-researchers. The network is not "anti-police"—in fact, charter members include police officers who understand the problem from the inside—but rather anti-copaganda, and pro-truth. The network came together in the belief that copaganda is in effect a Big Lie that has become so dominant in our country that it has had demonstrably negative impacts on our political system and our policy approach to public safety, justice, and criminal legal matters. It has distorted municipal, state, and national budgets, promoted a mythological link between safety and police, and led to a group of armed agents of the state roaming our streets free to do as they please. Copaganda needs to be abolished.

The way things are is not the way things have to be. We have choices to make and worlds to build. And none of this is possible in the absence of collective action and a social movement for radical transformation—we need to work collectively on a vision as part of the fight for abolition. We can abolish the ironclad logic of *misbehavior = police = punishment = the cage*, which leads onward and downward without end, and replace it with a logic of compassion and repair with incarceration as the last and least worthy alternative before us. Think of prison as the 1001st option—the last resort and not the default choice. We begin to frame the problem in different terms: recovery and restoration, forgiveness and redemption, grace and healing, public health and human rights, respect and faith. Alternatives liberate all of us from our own culturally imposed mental prisons, our dimmed consciousness and constrained imaginations. Without alternative ways of thinking and being, we become destined to be confined in a lockup state of mind.

Perhaps because we've lived so long in a culture of discipline and punish, or because copaganda has been so effective, or because traditional Puritanism became ravenous once again and demanded to be fed, or because our go-to-jail complex developed obsessive-compulsive disorder linked to attention-deficit hyperactivity—for these and other reasons, many folks hardly noticed as we slipped down the proverbial slope that Angela Davis, Ruthie Gilmore, Erica Meiners, Bernardine Dohrn, Beth Richie, and Dylan Rodriguez predicted, and we woke up living in a full-blown prison nation. That fact points to the true and deep-seated reason underneath the phenomenon of mass incarceration: white supremacy dressed up in modern garb. The system has been dubbed "the new Jim Crow" by the brilliant lawyer and scholar/activist Michelle Alexander, who points out that there are now more Black men in prison or on probation or parole than there were living in bondage as chattel slaves in 1850; that there are significantly more people caught up in the system of incarceration and supervision in America today—over six million folks—than inhabited Stalin's gulag at its height; that the American gulag constitutes the second largest city in this country, and that while the United States is less than 5 percent of the world's people, it holds over 25 percent of the world's combined prison population; that in the past twenty years the amount states have spent on prisons has risen six times the rate spent on higher education; and that on any given day tens of thousands of men, overwhelmingly Black and Latino, are held in the torturous condition known as solitary confinement.[8]

Just as slavery was a defining fact of American life from the seventeenth to the nineteenth centuries, racialized captivity and mass incarceration is a central feature in the US today. And just as the abolition of slavery was unimaginable to most Americans then, a society with no prisons or no police is difficult for many people to wrap their heads around now. But try it— imagine a world without prisons. When enough of us become liberated from the dogma of incarceration and the totalizing logic of captivity and control, we might mobilize ourselves to dive into the hard work of building a political movement to empty the prisons and shut them down. We may look back, just as we look back at slavery, with astonishment and anguish as we realize that the prison-industrial complex was a bad choice: it generated super-profits for a few while it vitalized white supremacy, ruined millions of human lives, devastated social capital, destroyed entire communities, and diminished our society. Slavery—the "peculiar institution"—made cruelty customary and callousness conventional, everyone forced to witness and embrace it as such, or to shut their eyes tight as communities were made more hard-hearted and hateful. Just as the abolition of slavery liberated enormous energy toward a more generous and compassionate social order, so a world without prisons will create the conditions for a more just and decent community for all.

Bernardine and I were in Montgomery, Alabama, on April 26, 2018, for the opening of the monumental National Memorial for Peace and Justice, commemorating the Black victims of lynching. The memorial is breathtaking, acknowledging past racial terrorism and advocating for racial and social justice. A few years earlier, we had visited the Museu Do Aljube in Lisbon with our dear Chicago friends James Thindwa from Zimbabwe and Martha Biondi. The museum is housed in the old prison where thousands of political prisoners and anticolonial freedom fighters were jailed and tortured during the dictatorship. We were moved and we were inspired. "Onward," James said, fist in the air. Let's build a world where one day our children or our grandchildren will visit the Museum of Mass Incarceration, the Museum of the Cops, and the Museum of Capitalism.

The brilliant geographer and intrepid abolitionist Ruth Wilson Gilmore argues that the abolitionists of today, standing on the shoulders of the abolitionists who preceded us, are required to change just one thing: *everything*. Abolition is best understood not as a deletion or an erasure but rather as a collection of creative and complex acts of "world-building."[9] What kind of world would we need to build in order to have no slavery? our forebears asked. And what kind of world could we begin to create today that would render prisons and police and militarism obsolete, predation and exploitation relics of a cruel past? To do that, everything would have to change. Everything.

And abolition work—changing everything—is the practice of freedom.

THANKS AND RECOGNITION

My initial inspiration to write this book came from a conversation I had with my comrade and friend Howard Waitzkin. My intention was to write something I could contribute to his marvelous series of pamphlets/manifestos called "Moving Beyond Capitalism—Now!" My next writing project will try do just that, focusing on postcapitalist schooling and linked in concrete ways to the ideas sketched out here.

My sincere thanks to comrades/collaborators Damon Williams and Daniel Kisslinger from the generative podcast AirGo and the dazzling media hub Respair Production and Media, as well as all those friends and comrades who read this as a work in progress and offered me your thoughtful notes: Rachel DeWoskin, Zayd Dohrn, Rick Ayers, Kevin Kumashiro, Howard Waitzkin, Wayne Au, Dayton Martingale, Julie Fain, Firoze Manji, Peter Clapp, Carole Saltz, Eleanor Stein, Lisa Lee, Adam Bush, and Bernardine Dohrn.

Deep appreciation to the smart and dedicated people at Beacon Press for "shining light on the past, spotlighting what matters in the present, and guiding us toward a better world": Gayatri Patnaik, Perpetua Charles, Claire Desroches, Alyssa Hassan, Rebecca Johnson, Susan Lumenello, Pamela MacColl, Emily Shelton, and especially my dazzling editor, Rachael Marks.

NOTES

AUTHOR'S NOTE

1. US House of Representatives, House Armed Services Committee, *Summary of the Fiscal Year 2023 National Defense Authorization Act,* https://democrats-armedservices.house.gov/_cache/files/c/8/c891c085-1494-4854-bb28-d145ea24ee99/C2675EB2D76A24A2A90546C41E6E993C.20220701-fy23ndaa-bill-summary-vfinal.pdf.

2. US Census Bureau, https://www.census.gov/en.html, accessed October 16, 2023.

3. Jane Hirshfield, "Telescope, Well Bucket, Furnace: Poetry Beyond the Classroom," *Writer's Chronicle,* March/April 2003.

4. Elizabeth Alexander, "The Black Poet as Canon-Maker: Langston Hughes and the Road to *New Negro Poets: USA,*" Poetry Foundation, February 2, 2007, https://www.poetryfoundation.org/articles/68438/the-black-poet-as-canon-maker.

5. Walt Whitman, "Song of Myself," *Leaves of Grass,* 1855.

1 WHEN FREEDOM IS THE QUESTION . . .

1. Mary Oliver, "Invitation," in *A Thousand Mornings* (New York: Penguin, 2013).

2. Viet Than Nguyen, *The Committed* (New York: Grove Press, 2021).

3. John Lewis, "Speech at the March on Washington," 1963.

4. Taína Asili, "Abolition," from *Abolition,* dir. Asili and Social Justice Initiative Portal Project, released October 8, 2021, https://sji.uic.edu/abolition/.

5. Paulo Freire, *Pedagogy of the Oppressed* (1968) (New York: Penguin, 2017).

6. Mariame Kaba and Kelly Hayes, *Let This Radicalize You: Organizing and the Revolution of Reciprocal Care (Abolitionist Papers)* (Chicago: Haymarket Books, 2023).

7. Langston Hughes, *The Panther & the Lash* (New York: Vintage Classics, 1967).

8. Martin Luther King, "Address at Riverside Church," New York, 1967.

9. Abraham Lincoln, First Inaugural Address, 1861.

10. William Wordsworth, "To Toussaint L'Ouverture," 1802, lines 13–14, https://www.bartleby.com/lit-hub/library/poem/to-toussaint-louverture/.

11. Abraham Lincoln, Second Inaugural Address, 1865.

12. Asili, "Abolition."

13. Fred Moten and Stefano Harney, *The University and the Undercommons: Seven Theses* (Durham, NC: Duke University Press, 2004, 114).

2 IMAGINE A WORLD THAT COULD BE—BUT IS NOT YET

1. Henry David Thoreau, *Civil Disobedience* (1849) (London: Simple Life Press, 1903).

2. Frederick Douglass, *My Bondage and My Freedom* (New York: Penguin, 2003).

3. *The Black Panther Party: Vanguard of the Revolution*, dir. Stanley Nelson, 2015.

4. Maxine Greene, *The Dialectic of Freedom* (New York: Teachers College Press, 1988), 15, 86.

5. Greene, *The Dialectic of Freedom*, 15, 86.

6. Martin Luther King Jr., "Beyond Vietnam," Speech at Riverside Church Meeting, New York, April 4, 1967.

7. Frederick Douglass, "What to the Slave Is the Fourth of July?," 1852.

8. NAACP, "Criminal Justice System Corrections," Criminal Justice Fact Sheet, https://naacp.org/resources/criminal-justice-fact-sheet, accessed October 17, 2023.

9. Bertolt Brecht, "A Worker Reads History," *Svendborg Poems* (New York: Grove Press, 1947).

10. Mariame Kaba, "One Million Experiments," https://millionexperiments.com.

11. Eduardo Galeano, personal correspondence, Chicago, 2000.

12. "What Life Means to Einstein: An Interview by George Sylvester Viereck," *The Saturday Evening Post*, October 26, 1929, 117, https://www.saturdayeveningpost.com/wp-content/uploads/satevepost/what_life_means_to_einstein.pdf.

13. Emily Dickinson, "XXVII," in *The Single Hound: Poems of a Lifetime* (Boston: Little, Brown, 1914).

3 "LADY FREEDOM AMONG US"

1. Emma Lazarus, "The New Colossus," 1883.

2. Ralph Ellis and Greg Botelho, "CNN Exclusive: Rancher Says He's Not Racist, Still Defiant over Grazing Battle," CNN.com, April 24, 2014, https://www.cnn.com/2014/04/24/politics/cliven-bundy-interview/index.html.

3. Amir Vera and Laura Ly, "White Woman Who Called Police on a Black Man Birdwatching in Central Park Has Been Fired," CNN.com, May 26, 2020, https://www.cnn.com/2020/05/26/us/central-park-video-dog-video-african-american-trnd/index.htm.

4. Herman Melville, *Benito Cereno, Putnam's Monthly*, 1855.

5. Sly & the Family Stone, "Everyday People," released November 30, 1968.

6. Rabbi Hillel (Pirkei Avot 1:14).

7. Ronald Reagan, "Inaugural Address," 1981.

8. Margaret Thatcher, "Interview for '*Woman's Own*,'" September 23, 1987, Margaret Thatcher Foundation: Speeches, Interviews, Other Statements, https://www.margaretthatcher.org/document/106689.

9. Norman Geras, *The Contract of Mutual Indifference: Political Philosophy After the Holocaust* (New York: Verso, 1999).

10. Rudd Center for Food Policy and Health, "Food Marketing," Research, University of Connecticut, 2017, https://uconnruddcenter.org/research/food-marketing/.

11. US Department of Agriculture, "Food Security in the U.S.," https://www.ers.usda.gov/topics/food-nutrition-assistance/food-security-in-the-u-s/key-statistics-graphics, accessed October 18, 2023.

12. Mark Bittman, "Why Your New Year's Diet Is Doomed," *New York Times*, January 9, 2021, https://www.nytimes.com/2021/01/09/opinion/diet-resolution-new-years.html.

13. Mark Twain, "Free Speech Is for the Grave," in *The Privilege of the Grave*, 1906.

14. George Saunders, *A Swim in a Pond in the Rain: In Which Four Russians Give a Master Class on Writing, Reading, and Life* (New York: Penguin Random House, 2021).

15. *Sorry to Bother You*, dir. Boots Riley, 2018.

4 NO GODS, NO MASTERS

1. Manolis Glezos, personal correspondence, 2012.

2. Fyodor Dostoevsky, *The Grand Inquisitor* (1880).

3. Ray Bradbury, *Fahrenheit 451* (New York: Simon & Schuster, 1951).

4. Brian Baggins, "Mikhail Bakunin Biography," https://www.marxists.org/reference/archive/bakunin/bio, accessed October 18, 2023.

5. William Golding, *Lord of the Flies* (1954) (New York: Penguin, 2006).

6. Kenzaburo Oe, *Nip the Buds, Shoot the Kids* (New York: Grove Press, 1958).

7. Samuel Beckett, *Worstward Ho* (New York: Grove Press, 1983).

8. Dahr Jamail, "'The Wind Knows Your Name': Dahr Jamail on William Rivers Pitt," *Truthout*, https://truthout.org/articles/the-wind-knows-your-name-dahr-jamail-on-william-rivers-pitt, accessed October 18, 2023.

9. Muriel Rukeyser, "Käthe Kollwitz," 1960, lines 25–26, https://www
.poetryfoundation.org/poems/90874/kathe-kollwitz.

10. Haruki Murakami, *Colorless Tsukuru Tazaki and His Years of Pilgrim-age* (New York: Vintage, 2015).

11. Hannah Arendt, *Eichmann in Jerusalem: A Report on the Banality of Evil* (New York: Viking Press, 1963), 33.

5 TRUTH AND RECONCILIATION AND FREEDOM

1. Bertolt Brecht, *Galileo*, edited and with an introduction by Eric Bentley (1938) (New York: Grove Press, 1966), 32.

2. Galileo Galilei, *Starry Messenger*, 1610.

3. Brecht, *Galileo*, 17.

4. Fyodor Dostoevsky, *The Grand Inquisitor* (1880).

5. Karl Marx, "So-Called Primitive Accumulation," in *Capital*, 1867.

6. W. E. B. Du Bois, *Black Reconstruction in America* (New York: Free Press, 1998).

7. James Baldwin, *The Creative Process* (New York: Ridge Press, 1962).

8. José Saramago, *Blindness* (New York: Harcourt Brace, 1995).

9. Michael Cooper and Marc Santora, "McCain Rebukes Giuliani on Waterboarding Remark," *New York Times*, October 26, 2007, https://www
.nytimes.com/2007/10/26/us/politics/26giuliani.html.

10. James Baldwin, *The Fire Next Time* (New York: Vintage, 1992).

11. US Department of State, "Secretary of State Madeleine K. Albright: Interview on NBC-TV," *The Today Show with Matt Lauer*, 1998, https://1997
-2001.state.gov/statements/1998/980219a.html, accessed October 19, 2023.

12. "Paul Robeson," from *The Essential Gwendolyn Brooks* (New York: Library of America, 2005).

13. Anthony Lewis, "The Kissinger Doctrine," *New York Times*, February 27, 1975, https://www.nytimes.com/1975/02/27/archives/the-kissinger-doctrine
.html.

14. Sven Lindqvist, *"Exterminate All the Brutes": One Man's Odyssey into the Heart of Darkness and the Origins of European Genocide* (New York: New Press, 1997).

15. Michel-Rolph Trouillot, *Silencing the Past: Power and the Production of History* (Boston: Beacon Press, 2015).

16. Zora Neale Hurston, *Barracoon: The Story of the Last "Black Cargo"* (New York: Amistad, 2018).

17. Robin D. G. Kelley, *Freedom Dreams: The Black Radical Imagination* (Boston: Beacon Press, 2003).

18. Edward W. Said, *Representations of the Intellectual: The 1993 Reith Lectures* (New York: Vintage, 1996).

19. E. V. Debs, "The Canton, Ohio Speech, Anti-War Speech," *The Call*, 1918, https://www.marxists.org/archive/debs/works/1918/canton.htm, accessed November 6, 2023.

6 STUDYING FREEDOM/TEACHING ABOLITION

1. Gwendolyn Brooks, "Boy Breaking Glass" from *Blacks* (Chicago: Third World Press, 1987).

2. Ron DeSantis, *The Courage to Be Free: Florida's Blueprint for America's Revival* (New York: Broadside Books, 2023).

3. Amy Simonson, "Florida Bill to Shield People from Feeling 'Discomfort' over Historic Actions by Their Race, Nationality or Gender Approved by Senate Committee," CNN.com, January 20, 2022, https://www.cnn.com/2022/01/19/us/florida-education-critical-race-theory-bill/index.html.

4. David Walker, *Appeal to the Colored Citizens of the World*, 1829.

5. Frederick Douglass, *Narrative of the Life of Frederick Douglass, An American Slave*, 1845.

6. Becky Sullivan, "With a Nod to *1984* a Federal Judge Blocks Florida's Anti-'Woke' Law in Colleges," NPR, https://www.npr.org/2022/11/18/1137836712/college-university-florida-woke-desantis-1984.

7. George Orwell, *1984* (1949) (New York: Signet Classics, 1961).

8. Sullivan, "With a Nod to *1984* a Federal Judge Blocks Florida's Anti-'Woke' Law in Colleges."

9. Ira Stoll, "Is Randi Weingarten Really 'The Most Dangerous Person in the World'?" *Education Next*, November 30, 2022, https://www.educationnext.org/is-randi-weingarten-really-the-most-dangerous-person-in-the-world.

10. David Diop, *At Night All Blood Is Black* (New York: Farrar, Straus & Giroux, 2020).

11. James Baldwin, "A Talk to Teachers," *Saturday Review*, October 16, 1963.

12. Juan Gonzalez, *Harvest of Empire: A History of Latinos in America* (New York: Penguin, 2022).

13. Emily Dickinson, "XXVII," in *The Single Hound: Poems of a Lifetime* (Boston: Little, Brown, 1915).

14. Gwendolyn Brooks, "The Chicago Picasso," 1967.

15. Charles Cobb, "Prospectus for a Summer Freedom School Program," *Freedom School Curriculum*, 1963, http://www.educationanddemocracy.org/FSCfiles/B_05_ProspForFSchools.htm, accessed October 24, 2023.

16. Anthony Conwright, "Freedom Schools for Today's Justice Movement," Learning for Justice, https://www.learningforjustice.org/magazine/spring-2023/freedom-schools-for-todays-justice-movement, accessed October 24, 2023.

17. Martin Luther King Jr., "Sermon at Temple Israel of Hollywood," February 26, 1965, available at https://www.americanrhetoric.com/speeches/mlktempleisraelhollywood.htm.

18. Fyodor Dostoevsky, *The Brothers Karamazov* (1880).

7 CREATING CRAWL SPACES FOR FREEDOM

1. Karl Marx, "Theses on Feuerbach," in *The German Ideology*, 1845.

2. Lewis Carroll, *Alice in Wonderland* (Oxford: Clarendon Press, 1865).

8 . . . ABOLITION IS THE ANSWER

1. James Baldwin, "A Talk to Teachers," *Saturday Review*, October 16, 1963.

2. Tamar Lewin, "Coal Curriculum Called Unfit for 4th Graders," *New York Times*, May 11, 2011, https://www.nytimes.com/2011/05/12/education/12coal.html.

3. Daniella Evans, *The Office of Historical Corrections: A Novella and Stories* (New York: Riverhead, 2020).

4. Harry Blackmun, "From the Legal Information Institute and Project Hermes," 1994, https://www.law.cornell.edu/supct/html/93-7054.ZA1.html, accessed October 25, 2023.

5. *Racially Charged: America's Misdemeanor Problem*, dir. Robert Greenwald, 2020, Brave New Films.

6. Economic Policy Institute, "Wage Theft Costs American Workers as Much as $50 Billion a Year," 2014, https://www.epi.org/press/wage-theft-costs-american-workers-50-billion; Criminal Justice Information Services Division, "Property Crime," 2019, https://ucr.fbi.gov/crime-in-the-u.s/2019/crime-in-the-u.s.-2019/topic-pages/property-crime, accessed October 25, 2023.

7. Alec Karakatsanis, comment on "Twitter," September 9, 2021, @equalityAlec, https://twitter.com/equalityAlec/status/143605396060806059396.

8. Michelle Alexander, *The New Jim Crow: Mass Incarceration in the Age of Colorblindness* (New York: New Press, 2012).

9. Ruth Wilson Gilmore, *Change Everything: Racial Capitalism and the Case for Abolition* (Chicago: Haymarket Books, forthcoming 2024).

CREDITS

Taina Asili, lyrics for "Abolition," by Taína Asili, TainaAsili.com.

Gwendolyn Brooks, "Boy Breaking Glass," "Chicago Picasso," and "Paul Robeson," from *The Essential Gwendolyn Brooks* (New York: Library of America, 2005). Copyright © 1970 by Gwendolyn Brooks. Reprinted by Consent of Brooks Permissions.

Roque Dalton, "Como tú/Like You," from *Poetry Like Bread: Poets of the Political Imagination*, ed. Martín Espada (Willimantic: Curbstone Press, 2000), pp. 128–29. Courtesy Northwestern University Press. All rights reserved.

Rita Dove, "Lady Freedom Among Us," first published in the *Congressional Record* 139, no. 148, Washington, DC © 1993 by Rita Dove. Reprinted by permission of the author.

Martín Espada, "Imagine the Angels of Bread," from *Imagine the Angels of Bread* by Martín Espada. Copyright © 1996 by Martín Espada. Used by permission of the author and W. W. Norton & Company, Inc.

June Jordan, "Poem Number Two on Bell's Theorem, or The New Physicality of Long-Distance Love," from *Directed by Desire: The Complete Poems of June Jordan*, Copper Canyon Press © Christopher D. Meyer, 2007. Reprinted by permission of the Frances Goldin Literary Agency.

James Oppenheim, "Bread and Roses," *The American Magazine*, December, 1911.

"Oh, Freedom" is a post–Civil War African American freedom song by an unknown artist.

"Woke Up This Morning with My Mind Stayed on Freedom" is adapted from "Woke Up This Morning with My Mind Stayed on Jesus," by Freedom Rider Rev. Robert Wesby.

INDEX

Abbott, Greg, 51
abolition: Civil War era, 8–10; as a
  creative process, 12, 136; erad-
  ication/removal components,
  11–12; impacts, 126; raising
  abolitionist children, 119–23;
  reading list, 93; self-liberation,
  9; world-building goal, 12. *See
  also* Black Freedom Movement;
  freedom; police abolition;
  prison abolition
"Abolition" (Asili), 6
Adorno, Theodor, 33
advertising industry, 75–76, 121, 126
agency/empowerment: education
  and, x–xi, 91, 99, 116; moral
  courage, self-respect, 8, 15–18,
  50–51, 83, 88, 111; as necessary
  for freedom, 83; self-respect, 88;
  truth-telling, 56, 91; working
  for change, 4, 7, 15–18, 95–96.
  See also collective power;
  education
Albright, Madeleine, 73
Alexander, Michelle, 134
Alim, Malik, ix–x
Allen, James, 90
America: American dream myth,
  126–27; exceptionalism myth,
  73, 127; excuses for use of force,

73; foundational enslavement
  and genocide, 70, 72–73; foundational lawlessness, 68; honest
  origin story for, 68–70. *See also*
  capitalism; US government;
  violence; white supremacy
anarchism, collectivist/socialist,
  51–52, 123. *See also* participatory democracy
Anderson, Jourdan, 80–81
Anderson, Marian, 4
the Anthropocene, 59–60, 83
*Appeal to the Colored Citizens of the
  World* (Walker), 89
Arendt, Hannah, 59
art/creativity: and courage, 91,
  161; and imagining freedom,
  3–5, 91–92; pain from, 92; role
  in expanding the imagination, 25–26. *See also* freedom
  dreams; imagination; poetry
Asili, Taína, 6, 12
authoritarianism, 2, 44–45, 71

Bakunin, Mikhail, 51
Baldwin, James: on America's history, 121; "A Talk to Teachers,"
  90; on truth-telling, 69; on
  white supremacy, 73
Barracoon (Hurston), 80

prison abolition: changes needed for, 56–57; imagining, 135–36; logic of, 128; steps for moving towards, 130–31; working collectively toward, 134. *See also* mass incarceration
property crimes, 132–33
Purdue Pharma, 18–19

questioning. *See* interrogating the world

racial capitalism, 23
Reagan, Ronald, 37–38
refugees, 90–91
repair: as an alternative to incarceration, 130, 134; authentic, 30; as a requirement for reconciliation, 79–80; Sherman's "forty acres and a mule" promise, 82, 126. *See also* reparations
reparations, 10, 23, 30, 80–81, 102, 112
restorative truth, 78
retribution, revenge, 10, 128
Richards, BJ, 121
Richie, Beth, 128, 134
Riley, Boots, 45
Rukeyser, Muriel, 57

Saramago, Jose, 70
Sartre, Jean-Paul, 66–67
Saunders, George, 44–45
Schenwar, Maya, 120
school shootings, 75
Schwerner, Mickey, 37, 94
settler colonialism, xiii, 22, 68, 75
Sherman, William Tecumseh, 82
Simone, Nina, 8, 110
slavery. *See* chattel slavery
SNCC (Student Nonviolent Coordinating Committee), 3–4, 50, 93–94, 97

society (collective social order): reinforcing the existing order, 86–87; vs. toxic individualism, 37–40; and white supremacy, 31
Sorkin, Aaron, 127–28
Sorry to Bother You (film, Riley), 45
"Starry Messenger" (Galileo), 65
Sterling, Donald, 32
Stewart, Sylvester (Sly and the Family Stone), 35
Stovall, Dave, 115
strategy, 113–14
structural inequities/racism, xi, 16, 19, 30–32, 39, 59, 91, 94, 100
Student Nonviolent Coordinating Committee. *See* SNCC (Student Nonviolent Coordinating Committee)

tactics, 114–15
"A Talk to Teachers" (Baldwin), 90
teaching. *See* education
theocracy, 87
Thindawa, James, 135–36
This Nonviolent Stuff'll Get You Killed (Cobb), 20
Thoreau, Henry David, 15
Trouillot, Michel-Rolph, 78
Truth and Reconciliation Commission (TRC), South Africa, 80
truth-telling: historical truth, 78; importance of, 68–70, 73, 109; and manipulating truth, 75–76; and reconciliation, 79–80; revolutionary nature of, 64–65; and science, 76–77; types of truth, 77–78
Tubman, Harriet, 9, 18
Twain, Mark, 41–42

Under the Tree: A Seminar on Freedom (podcast), ix–x

unfreedom: defining freedom using, 3, 89; identifying, 15, 20–22, 30, 91; importance of education for getting to roots of, 91; and misuse of the term "freedom," 89; resisting, 15–18, 24; structural, implications of, 30. *See also* education

US government: emphasis on the individual, 30; and the interchangeability of democracy and domination, 74; militarism, 19–20, 22, 75, 83, 128; National Defense Authorization Act (2023), ix

Viet Thanh Nguyen, 3

violence: vs. nonviolence, as a false dichotomy, 18–20; public-health frame for, 131; settler colonialism, xiii, 9, 83; structural racism, 16, 19, 94, 100. *See also* mass incarceration

wage slavery, 45–46
wage theft, 132–33
Walker, David, 89
Wesby, Robert, 85
white supremacy: and mass incarceration, 128; recognizing as an unfreedom, 21–23; as the theme of *Benito Cereno*, 33–35; willful blindness about, 31–32, 69–70. *See also* chattel slavery; structural inequities/racism
Whitman, Walt, x–xi
Without Sanctuary (Allen), 90
woke, as a term, 88
"Woke Up This Morning with My Mind Stayed on Freedom" (Wesby), 85
Woodfox, Albert, 112, 128
Wordsworth, William, 9
Worstward Ho (Beckett), 55
Writing Our Lives class, 104–5

Zhou Enlai, 78